RUSSIAN LITERATURE

IN TRANSLATION 1

SIDNEY MONAS, EDITOR

Gumilev, sketched by N. Goncharova in 1917. From Gumilev, *Sobranie sochinenii,* vol. 4 (frontispiece).

SELECTED WORKS OF

Nikolai S. Gumilev

SELECTED & TRANSLATED

BY BURTON RAFFEL

AND ALLA BURAGO

WITH AN INTRODUCTION

BY SIDNEY MONAS

STATE UNIVERSITY OF NEW YORK PRESS

ALBANY · 1972

Selected Works of Nikolai S. Gumilev

First Edition

Published by State University of New York Press
99 Washington Avenue, Albany, New York 12210

Library of Congress Cataloging in Publication Data

Gumilev, Nikolaĭ Stepanovich, 1886–1921.
  Selected works of Nikolai S. Gumilev.

  (Russian literature in translation, 1)
    I. Raffel, Burton, tr. II. Burago, Alla, tr. III. Series.
PG3476.G85A27   891.7′1′42   74–161442
ISBN 0–87395–098–4
ISBN 0–87395–198–0 (microfiche)

Printed in the United States of America
Designed by Richard Hendel

Contents

* The dates given here are dates of composition, not of publication.

Stories

Drama

Literary Criticism

Preface

This is the first volume of a series called Russian Literature in Translation.

It is designed to bring much that is unknown or known only through very inadequate translations into the midst of those who read and write English. Therefore the works and authors that appear in this series will be relatively little known to the non-Russian reader, and since the basis of choice will be the editor's notion of what has been important and exciting in Russian literature, even the Russian reader may on occasion be surprised.

The great novels of Tolstoy and Dostoevsky will not be included. I do not underestimate their importance to world literature and I am well aware of the need for fresh, and better, translations. But Russian literature has too often been approached as though there were little else. And whatever the deficiencies of existing Tolstoy-Dostoevsky translations, they have not been so gross as to block fundamental access to these authors.

With poetry it is altogether a different matter. Pushkin is of course a name. In the last few years, I have been able to count at least six English translations of *Evgeny Onegin*. Not one of them gives an adequate notion of the original, but perhaps studying them together, along with the superb notes provided by Vladimir Nabokov for his insistently literal version, the exceptionally diligent reader may acquire some notion of the world of Onegin. But it would probably be easier for him to learn at least enough Russian to be able to use Nabokov's translation as a trot.

There has been some interest in Pushkin's prose. A few of the lyric poems have appeared in anthologies and collections. I remember being particularly struck by the eloquence of an early Pushkin lyric translated into Lalands dialect by Sydney Goodsir Smith. And there have been a few poems rendered by Vladimir Nabokov and perhaps a handful of others, among them translations by Burton Raffel in his anthology, *Russian Poetry under the Tsars,* that may be read as English poems. On the whole, in spite of the long wail of Russianists, Pushkin is very little read in English.

Then there is the matter of the Silver Age. The period from 1895 to about 1921 is called the Silver Age of Russian literature by most scholars, an almost unprecedented flowering of all the arts in Russia in close relationship with each other—music, dance, painting and theater as well as poetry and fiction. Historical, religious, and political thought and literary and art criticism of a very high order also flourished. It was the period during which Russian literature was most receptive to European currents in the arts and during which it had in turn its greatest impact upon them. Whatever the relationship of individual artists to the political upheaval of 1917 to 1921, the art of the period as art tended to be radical, innovative, and extreme and therefore in a real sense revolutionary.

It is not intended that this series be limited to poetry or to the Silver Age alone. But that does seem like a good place to start. In general, my notion of what constitutes literature will be a broad one: not merely poetry, fiction, and literary criticism; but anything of literary quality, including the rich veins of Russian memoirs and historical and religious thought. Every volume will include an interpretive essay and notes where, with the intelligent general reader in mind, these seem useful.

Within the Silver Age, the literary school known as Acmeism seems to be a good place to begin this series, and within this school, it makes sense to start with Nikolai Gumilev, who, though not the greatest of the Acmeists, was the founder and teacher of the group which included two of the most eloquent poets of the twentieth century, Osip Mandelstam and Anna Akhmatova (poets whose works I hope will soon follow in this series). Gumilev is an interesting poet and a talented critic. His work points both to the past, especially in the direction of Pushkin, and to the future, in that in his enormously important role as a publicist and teacher as well as by the example of his own work, he persuaded and helped young Russian poets to study and master their craft and, somewhat in the manner of Ezra Pound whose contemporary he was, to "make it new."

The volume includes a representative selection of his work. I believe it is the first such volume available to the English reader. The Russian reader, since the work is presented from a distinctly American and contemporary point of view, should find it interesting as well.

Something remains to be said about the problem of translation, especially the translation of poetry. As everyone knows, it is impossible. Yet it must be done. On that assumption, we have proceeded.

Burton Raffel, a gifted American poet, is a splendid and experienced translator, as readers of his *Beowulf,* his translations of the Indonesian poet Chairil Anwar, and his anthology of pre-Revolutionary Russian poetry already know. He has worked from languages he knows well, only a little, and (with the help of a collaborator) scarcely at all, as is the case with Russian. His collaborator here has been Alla Burago, a young Russian scholar who is completely and equally at home in Russian and English, and who has a very strong feeling for the possibilities of both languages. Mr. Raffel has been the poet; but Miss Burago has shown an unusual awareness of and sensitivity to what a translating poet needs to know about the original.

In addition to his poetic ability and in correlation with his skill in translation, Mr. Raffel is a provocative and inspired theorist of translation (his book, *The Forked Tongue,* should attest to this). The idea for this series was born of our discussions about the nature of translation and about the general need for translations from the Russian.

Mr. Raffel laid down the principles of selection for this volume (the idea of translating Gumilev's works was his). Miss Burago selected material according to these principles, and from among these Professor Raffel made further selections. Miss Burago checked his work against the original Russian, and he rewrote on the basis of her emendations. At this stage, I reviewed their work, in some instances making further suggestions and also proposing new material for inclusion. The three of us agreed upon the final contents. Such is the manner and extent of our collaboration. The final checking of the manuscript was my responsibility. If, then, any errors have persisted, the blame is mine.

Our ideal in any case has been poetry and prose which may be read and judged as English poetry and prose while still remaining essentially faithful, both in spirit and in detail, to the Russian text.

Gumilev is a master of conventional Russian meters. Mr. Raffel's poems are much freer. In most places he has used irregular meter and only occasional rhyme. It is not Gumilev's formal devices that he has sought to translate, and his poems should be read independently as English poems. Yet I believe even the Russian reader will be struck by their closeness in tone and detailed content to the original.

Prose is not always easier to translate than poetry. In the case of Gumilev, who wrote a poet's prose, it is strikingly the reverse. I believe that the Raffel-Burago translation of Gumilev's prose will be seen in this connection to be of exceptional merit.

To the energy, resourcefulness, good nature, and intelligently critical receptivity of the translators I feel I owe a debt of personal gratitude. Both the translators and I owe as well a great deal to Gleb Struve and Boris Filipoff, without whose magnificent Russian edition of Gumilev it would have been very difficult indeed to put together this collection. I would myself like to thank George Ivask for his shrewd comments and advice, and Mrs. Gianna Kirtley, who helped a great deal.

Sidney Monas

Introduction

by Sidney Monas

Gumilev

AKMÊ AND ADAM IN SAINT PETERSBURG

Nikolai Stepanovich Gumilev was born in April 1886, in the naval hospital of the island fortress of Kronstadt, the key to Saint Petersburg harbor. His mother was a Princess L'vov and she had a brother who was an admiral. In the time of Nicholas I, a half-century earlier, a Prince L'vov had composed the Russian national anthem.

Gumilev's father was a naval surgeon, a man of dignified, severe appearance, but inwardly insecure, who had married (she was his second wife) a woman much above him socially and twenty years his junior. The family name derived from the Latin *humilis,* indicating clerical origins. At school, during roll call, when his name was read with the accent on the first syllable, tending in Russian to emphasize the etymology, young Nikolai Stepanovich would refuse to rise. Humble he never was.

He had an elongated head that looked, as a friend put it, as if the midwife's tongs had pulled too hard. Shrewd eyes squinted from either side of a fleshy, shapeless nose. His lips were thick and pale. He lisped. "Awkwardness, with great difficulty overcome," his friends summed up the essential character under the elegant veneer of his later assured, masterful, magisterial pose.[1]

Even before he went to school, he began to write fables. At the age of eight, he wrote his first poems. His family moved from the suburb of Tsarskoe Selo to Saint Petersburg to Tiflis (in Georgia) and then back to Tsarskoe Selo. In Tiflis, he published his first poems (he was fourteen) and went through, as did so many young Russian intellectuals of that time, a Marxist conversion, the traces of which, however, seem to have disappeared by the time he returned north with his family in 1903.

At nineteen, his first book appeared. At twenty-five, he was the ac-

---

1. Any study of Gumilev must begin and end with the definitive edition of his collected works, edited by Gleb Struve and Boris Filipoff: N. Gumilev, *Sobranie sochinenii,* 4 vols. (Washington, D.C., 1962–1968). This edition contains all the published works, the known manuscripts, including variant versions. It includes letters, fragments from diaries, accounts, ample annotations, a splendid bibliography, and excellent essays by the editors and by V. M. Sechkarev and V. Veidle (W. Weidlé). Professor Struve's biographical introduction to volume 1 is a model of fairness and conciseness. In addition I have relied heavily on Nikolai Otsup's preface (he was Gumilev's personal friend and disciple) to his edition of Gumilev's selected works, *Izbrannoe* (Paris, 1959); and Sergei Makovsky, *Na parnasse "serebrianogo veka"* (Munich, 1962), pp. 195–222. I have also used A. A. Gumileva, "Nikolai Stepanovich Gumilev," *Novyi Zhurnal,* no. 46 (1956), pp. 107–26 and V. Nevedomskaia, "Vospominaniia o Gumileve i Akhmatovoi," *Novyi Zhurnal,* no. 38 (1954), pp. 182–90.

Gumilev's father. From Gumilev, *Sobranie sochinenii,* 4:528.

knowledged master of an important literary movement, the hero of the youthful avant-garde. In between, he had studied Romance philology in Paris and Saint Petersburg but had also, and with considerable daring and enterprise, explored Africa. He acquired a reputation as a Don Juan, and women fell at his feet. But the "simple, arrogant dream" of Don Juan (as he called it in an early poem, see p. 42)—though it recurred throughout his life—could not satisfy him:

> . . . never father to a woman's child,
> never any man's brother.

He married a strong, deep woman, one of the great poets of the twentieth century, Anna Akhmatova. Their relationship was a stormy one and, in 1918, ended in divorce. But it had far greater impact on the work of both, and in this sense far greater significance, than the more lurid and more publicized "time of troubles" between Esenin and Isadora Duncan.

In 1914, at twenty-eight, Gumilev enlisted in the war. He was the only well-known Russian poet to fight in the front lines. His war poems have been compared with those of Charles Peguy (which they really did resemble) and with those of Kipling and D'Annunzio (which they did not). At thirty, he had been twice awarded the Order of Saint George, Imperial Russia's highest combat decoration for bravery. At the war's end, he was in Paris, having volunteered to fight with the Allies on the Salonika front but caught in the maze of Allied bureaucracies.[2] By that time, the Bolsheviks had been in power in Petrograd a full year. Although Gumilev was a monarchist and made no bones about it, he chose to return, making his way back through Stockholm where he wrote a memorable poem about homecoming (see "Stockholm," p. 90).

Arriving in Red Petrograd in 1918, he began to teach young proletarian poets the craft of verse. All accounts agree that he was a splendid teacher. He also became involved in a curious partnership with Maxim Gorky, who was then using his great prestige with the Bolsheviks to try to keep the Russian intelligentsia alive. The device that Gorky adapted for this purpose was one that also came naturally to an autodidact of great erudition like himself, with his enormous respect for the educative and moral uplift of the written word—a grandiose project for making the classics of world literature available in Russian translation to a broad audience. The Bolsheviks provided the funds and (more

2. For an account of Gumilev in Paris, see Victor Serge, *Memoirs of a Revolutionary, 1901–1941* (London: Oxford Paperbacks, 1967), pp. 59–60.

Akhmatova, drawn by Modigliani in 1911. From Anna
Akhmatova, *Sobranie sochinenii,* ed. Gleb Struve and
Boris Filipoff (Washington, D. C., 1965), 1:48.

Gumilev and Akhmatova, with Lev (1915?). Born in 1911,
Lev, the son of the two poets, is today a distinguished
orientalist. From Anna Akhmatova, *Sobranie sochinenii,*
2:48.

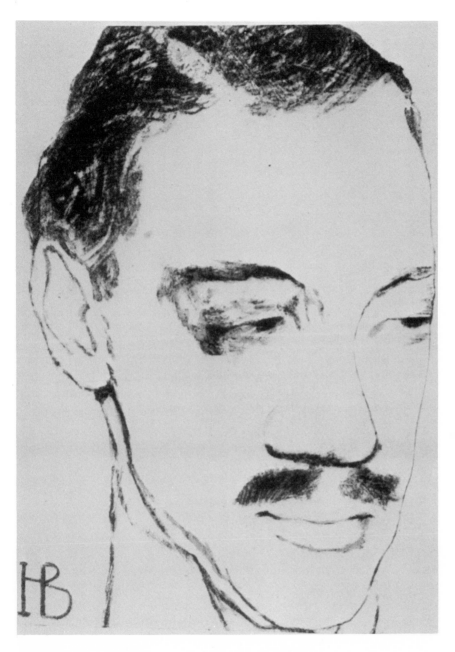

Gumilev, sketched by N. Voinitskaya in 1909. From
S. Makovsky, *Na parnase "serebrianogo veka"* (Munich, 1962),
p. 194.

important) the rations that enabled poets, novelists, and professors to keep themselves alive during the difficult years of the Civil War by working on translations. Alexander Blok, the great symbolist poet who had tried to respond affirmatively to the Revolution and failed, close to despair and physical and spiritual exhaustion, looked with a somber and somewhat jaundiced eye on the young reactionary and the famous radical working together and discovered in their solemn world-improving earnestness a common bond others might not have suspected. "Gumilev and Gorky," Blok wrote in his diary:

> Their resemblances. On the deliberate side, a distaste for Fet and Polonsky—each in his own way, of course. No matter how little love lost there is between them, they have something in common. Neither knows anything about tragedy—about ambivalent truths. Both are northeasterners.[3]

In the summer of 1921, Petrograd still smoldered with the afterglow of the Kronstadt uprising. Just as the Civil War had been substantially won and the White opposition destroyed, just as the policy of appeasement and compromise with the peasantry and small-scale entrepreneurship known as the New Economic Policy, or NEP, was about to be launched, a left-wing but anti-Bolshevik revolt broke out in what had been regarded as the stronghold of the Revolution. For it was among the sailors of Kronstadt that the Bolsheviks had drawn their first and their best forces—the shock troops of the Revolution and the Civil War. Therefore, signs which went up on the island-fortress urging Soviets without Bolsheviks! caused Lenin and Trotsky grave and prolonged anxiety. The capital had been moved from Petrograd to Moscow as a precaution against possible German siege. Still, Petrograd was the city of the Revolution, and Kronstadt was the key to Petrograd. Trotsky himself directed the attack on the island, and the revolt was ruthlessly suppressed. For some time, in that area, the Party and the Cheka were extremely skittish and touchy on the subject of counter-revolution and conspiracy, whether from the "anarchist" left or the right or the remnants of Provisional Government liberalism.

Under circumstances that are far from clear, Gumilev became involved in the so-called Tagantsev conspiracy. Sixty-one persons were arrested by the Cheka, among them a number of prominent members of the intelligentsia. From prison Gumilev wrote his second wife,

---

3. Alexander Blok, quoted in Gumilev, *Sobranie sochinenii,* 4:550 (the translation is my own). Fet and Polonsky were lyricists of great introspection, and at a time when the pure lyric was outside the mainstream of Russian literature.

Gumilev as a volunteer in the Uhlan Bodyguard Regiment,
1915. From Gumilev, *Sobranie sochinenii,* vol. 4, opposite
p. 440.

"Don't worry about me. I'm well, writing verses and playing chess." [4]
He is said, in prison, to have been reading Homer and the New Testament. Meanwhile, a number of his friends began frantically trying to locate him, but without success. On 21 August, at Blok's funeral (in death, at least, the two poets found a certain solidarity), a small group of Gumilev's friends attempted in a more organized manner to invoke "influential" help—the editors of publishing houses, and Gorky himself. To no avail; probably on 24 August (the exact date is not certain) he was shot by the Cheka at the age of thirty-five. [5]

THE Marquis de Custine, visiting Russia in 1839, had called Saint Petersburg a monument to Russia's future power. A peculiarly vulnerable and exposed monument, as it turned out, for with the rising power of Germany, the city that Peter the Great had built as fortress and base against the Swedes seemed more a pawn to the enemy than a bastion of defense. Within the city, modern industry and modern technology brought with them a modern proletariat, and against the background of a primitive hinterland that could hardly economically sustain it. As a monument to power, Saint Petersburg, Petrograd, showed many cracks, and the Bolsheviks quickly removed the base of their power to the more ancient capital of Moscow.

Peter had also intended the city as a center of commerce and civilization—his famed "window to the west." Within a century of its founding the city became a stage set not only for the drama of power but as well for those curious subplots called civilization and enlightenment, the future cultural mission of Russia's educated classes.

Saint Petersburg: the great seaport of a landlocked empire, rococo palaces resting on drained swampland periodically threatened by flood; city of the book trade, of university students, and the secret police; city of planned perspectives and *l'esprit geometrique,* with Paris on one side and Asia on the other; where the largest, the most capital-intensive, the most modern industry overshadowed grimy tenements in which peasant artisans tried to scrape a meager living from medieval handicrafts; "northern Palmyra" of summertime white nights and endless winter gloom; city of enlightenment-rationality and surrealist-hallucination; Peter the Great postmarked his letters from there *Rai*—"Heaven!";

4. Ibid., 1:xlii.
5. Bertram Wolfe, *The Bridge and the Abyss* (New York, 1967), pp. 121–32, makes a case to the effect that it was Gumilev's execution that precipitated Gorky's partial break with Lenin and impelled him to leave Russia for Capri. The authority for this is still mainly the writer Evgeny Zamiatin. Nikolai Otsup and also Nadezhda Mandelstam (in her recent memoir) claim to know nothing about this.

Pushkin cursed it but nonetheless dedicated himself to the fulfillment of its cultural mission. Where else could a sensitive Russian boy at the beginning of the twentieth century have dreamt of Africa and Montparnasse, captains and warriors, poets and saints, Byzantium and Eden? It was the Petersburg dream that Gumilev spent his life acting out.

Like Conrad and Rimbaud, he journeyed to Africa. But it was a literary Africa, "hanging like a great pear/on the ancient tree of Eurasia" (see "Prelude to *Tent*," p. 57), the Africa that "old maps used to show as a girl, rough and yet somehow beautiful" (see "African Hunt," p. 141). Gumilev's poem, "The Sahara," is an extended metaphor which compares in fine detail the vastness of ocean with the desolation of the desert, the waves of water with the waves of sand (see p. 58). It is no doubt based on first-hand observation. Yet Georgy Ivanov (whose reminiscences are sometimes fanciful, but rarely without point) reports that when he asked Gumilev what it was like to experience the Sahara for the first time, the latter replied, "I didn't notice it. I was sitting on a camel, reading Ronsard."[6] The capital of his literary empire was always Saint Petersburg. He was born in Kronstadt, and he died of it.

Gumilev grew up in Tsarskoe Selo, a suburb haunted by Pushkin, who had gone to school there, and ornamented by the magnificent summer palace designed by Rastrelli, and the parks surrounding it. Tsarskoe Selo—"the Tsar's Village." Alexander I had founded the lyceum that Pushkin attended mostly as a training school for statesmen and civil servants. A later schoolmaster of Tsarskoe Selo, Innokentii Annensky, translator of Euripides and one of Gumilev's most admired culture heroes, asked somberly in one of his poems, "Was it the Tsar's decree composed us all?"[7] Over all the splendid symmetry of rococo palaces and parks there hung the shadow of autocratic power, endowing the softest smiles of the sculpted cherubim with a certain melancholy noticeable for instance, though not directly mentioned, in Pushkin's quatrain on "A Tsarskoe Selo Statue":

Against the rock, the girl has shattered her urn and the water runs out.
Sadly the girl sits, holding a useless shard.
Strange! as it pours from the shattered urn, the water doesn't run dry;
Over an eternal stream, the girl sits, eternally sad.[8]

6. Georgy Ivanov, quoted in Gumilev, *Sobranie Sochinenii,* 1:xxvii.
7. Innokentii Annenskii, *Stikhotvoreniia i tragedii* (Leningrad, 1959), p. 199.
8. A. S. Pushkin, *Polnoe sobranie sochinenii* (Moscow, 1957), 3:180.

It is Tsarskoe Selo where, in his poem "Memory" (see p. 109), Gumilev sees himself as a lonely "witch-child" in distant perspective, and it is Petersburg, suggestive always of architectural metaphor, where he is the "stubborn architect/of this dark temple" (i.e., himself) and where, in a paraphrase from Blake,

> . . . the new Jerusalem's
> clear, pure walls rise
> in Russian fields.

It is from Tsarskoe Selo and Saint Petersburg that all Gumilev's voyages begin.

GUMILEV lived in a world of obstacles. At home, as a child, he had an older brother and a morose father to rival him for the attention of a young mother and a pretty girl cousin. Later, there were the Symbolists; and, above all, Alexander Blok. Conscious of his own homeliness and awkwardness, he was a performer, a surmounter, an overreacher. He cultivated the matter-of-fact ease of the tightrope walker and the assurance of the trapeze artist: the difficult and dangerous act carried through with unflappable *sang-froid*. Those who knew him well write nevertheless of his freshness of spirit and his childlike good nature, his utter lack of hatred or malice and his spontaneous enthusiasm and indefatigable energy as a teacher. It was a formidable pose in which he clothed himself, and it became a kind of second nature.

He was proud of difficulties overcome. The Symbolists groaned and suffered the difficulties of the literary life; before departing for Africa or the battlefield, Gumilev wrestled with the devices of poems, spread the works out on the table and put them back together again. His was a grimier, sweatier angel, he implied, and he was proud of it.

Having translated Theophile Gautier's "L'Art," Gumilev set himself in a chiseled, white-marble, Parnassian stance: balance, precision, clarity, craftsmanship, tradition, restraint. It required a Greek name, and he gave it one. *Akmê:* the peak, the ripening, the perfection. He called the "movement" Acmeism.[9]

Like Anglo-American Imagism, which it much resembles, Acmeism grew out of and at the same time opposed *fin de siècle Romanticism*. During the period between 1909 and 1913, a decadent Symbolism gave rise to two modernist movements, which, without it, could scarcely have existed, but which nevertheless deeply criticized and severely un-

9. H. W. Chalsma has written an excellent dissertation, unfortunately as yet unpublished, but available in microfilm, *Russian Acmeism: Its History, Doctrine, and Poetry* (Ann Arbor: University Microfilms, 1967).

dermined Symbolist themes, attitudes, and atmospheres: Acmeism and Futurism.

In their antagonistic relationship, Acmeism seemed to take the conservative, Futurism the radical position. Acmeism emphasized tradition and craftsmanship, clarity, balance, and understatement. Futurism, with Mayakovsky and Khlebnikov as its greatest representatives, studied provocation, Bohemian rebelliousness, innovation, and hyperbole. Gumilev called the Futurists hyenas in the track of the Symbolist lion (see 'Acmeism and the Legacy of Symbolism," p. 245). Vladimir Markov, a gifted critic, but very partial to Futurism, has recently written that if Gumilev had not had the bad luck to have been shot in the cellars of the Cheka, there would have been no need to invent Socialist Realism.[10]

Both Futurists and Acmeists, however, emphasized poetry as a craft, a thing made. Both saw it as a movement from the irrational to the rational: a bringing to consciousness. Both emphasized technique and a pragmatic, matter-of-fact, craftsmanly approach. The Formalist critics, who defined a work of art as "the sum of its devices," and who prided themselves both on their scientific approach to literature and their pragmatic approach to particular texts, although they have been traditionally associated with the Futurists, welcomed both Futurists and Acmeists as kindred spirits.[11]

Much of Gumilev's work, however, justifies Markov's suspicions. As another acute critic, George Ivask, has recently pointed out, many of his poems seem to lack a dimension. They work out too well, all too explicitly, their intended meaning.[12] Gumilev's insistence on and pride in "a firm, manly attitude," comes dangerously close to what we tend to see as a boy scout attitude, gotten up in somewhat supercrackly rhetoric. When we read of angel-wings hovering over soldiers on the battlefield, we tend to wince. He glorified:

> Explorers, discoverers,
> not frightened by hurricanes,
> at home with whirlpools and sandbars,

10. Vladimir Markov, "Mysli o russkom futurizme," *Novyi Zhurnal,* no. 38 (1954), p. 180.
11. Both Boris Eikhenbaum and Viktor Zhirmunsky (the latter not fully accepted by the Formalists as one of them but clearly quite close to their thinking) have written interestingly and appreciatively of the Acmeists: Boris Eikhenbaum, *Anna Akhmatova: Opyt Analiza* (Petrograd, 1923); V. Zhirmunsky, "O poezii klassicheskoi i romanticheskoi," "Dva napravleniia sovremennoi liriki," and "Preodolevshie simvolizm," three essays collected in his book, *Voprosy teorii literatury* (Leningrad, 1928).
12. Iurii Ivask, "Russkie poety: N. Gumilev," *Novyi Zhurnal,* no. 98 (1970), pp. 132-35.

Their hearts not stuffed with the dust
of forgotten manuscripts, but steeped in sea-salt,
setting a course with bold strokes
on a torn map, starting some daring voyage.[13]

The White armies are said to have memorized his poems and recited them in battle. The emigration, after his death, regarded him as a martyr. Although his poems have not been published in the USSR and his name, at least since the late 1920s, has rarely appeared in print there, he is nevertheless a favorite among Soviet youth, and in the current revival of Russian nationalism, or neo-Slavophilism as it is sometimes called, a movement which contains some quite loyal party members, his poetry plays a conspicuous role. He himself had boasted of the non-literary nature of his readers (see "My Readers," p. 125):

. . . strong, vicious, gay,
killers of elephants, killers of people,
dead in deserts,
frozen at the edge of eternal ice—
as it should be, on this
strong, gay, vicious planet—
and they carry my poems in their saddlebags.

Again, it is among those who understand true difficulty, not those contaminated by too-long exposure to "dusty manuscripts," that he wishes to be respected. He has been one of them himself.

I mean no disrespect to the dignity of the elemental in poetry or prose, but this particular posture of Gumilev's seems to me, as in Kipling, to hover close to the juvenile.

ALEXANDER BLOK was six years Gumilev's senior. While too great a poet to fit easily into any school, he belonged for a time to the Symbolists and many of his attitudes were characteristically Symbolist and characteristically those that Gumilev set himself to oppose. Of course, one must bear in mind that Gumilev rather liked slogans and banners and programs, while Blok tended to view them with distaste.

On the subject of literary translation—an interest both shared—Blok emphasized the importance of recreating the "atmosphere" of a poem. Gumilev, fond of prescriptions, listed nine characteristics and devices

---

13. Gumilev, "Kapitany," *Sobranie sochinenii*, 1:142. The complete poem is not included in the present volume. These lines have been translated by Burton Raffel and Alla Burago.

that must be transposed "unchanged" (see "On the Translation of Poetry," p. 238). Ironically, Gumilev's most eloquent translation, the Babylonian epic, *Gilgamesh*, violates almost everything he lists as "obligatory."

For Blok, inspiration sometimes meant a kind of possession by the muse. During one of those extraordinary encounters in the House of Art during the time of the Civil War, Gumilev argued that in Blok's famous poem about the Revolution, "The Twelve," the figure of Christ at the end seemed out of place, false and distasteful. Blok replied morosely that he, too, disliked it; but what could he do? In that way the poem had come to him.[14]

Blok's muse was obscure and uttered things sometimes incomprehensible to him. Gumilev's, on the other hand, spoke a language mutually understood, and he took it down.

For the Dionysian Blok, poetry was a dangerous descent into chaos in a quest for rebirth into the realm of the unconscious life of the instincts. Culture itself he called "the music by which the world grows." For the Apollonian Gumilev definiteness, clarity of line, sustenance of will were the virtues; one must not let go.

Blok was a Populist and believed in the masses. Gumilev, in praising Valery Briusov, a Symbolist, but the closest of all the Symbolists to Acmeism and a man Gumilev regarded as one of his masters, compared him to Peter the Great. Not by chance was Gumilev a monarchist.

Against Symbolism, Gumilev brought two major charges: that its emphasis on metaphor tended to produce a private and at the same time liturgical, a self-isolated language in which "like bees in a deserted hive / the dead words rot and stink" (see "The Word," p. 107) and that their quest for ultimate mystery involved the Symbolists in a whoring after strange gods, the theosophy and anthroposophy of Andrei Biely or the magic and Manicheism of Fyodor Sologub. For the Symbolists everything was something it wasn't. Every phenomenon, Gumilev insisted, had a right to exist (in poetry as in life) as and for itself. Or, in that so familiar phrase of Gertrude Stein's, "A rose is a rose is a rose." Osip Mandelstam, writing in 1922, in an essay which he begins with Gumilev's poem "The Word" (quoted above) as epigraph, wrote trenchantly and amusingly of the fix in which he felt Russian Symbolism had left Russian poetry. It is worth quoting at length:

Alles Vergaengliche ist nur ein Gleichnis. Let's take an example: a rose or the sun, a dove or a girl. For the Symbolist not one of

14. Gumilev, *Sobranie sochinenii,* 4:552.

these figures is interesting in itself; but rather, the rose is an image of the sun, the sun is an image of the rose, the dove is an image of the girl, and the girl is an image of the dove. The figures are gutted like a stuffed owl and packed with a strange content. Instead of a symbolic forest, a taxidermist's shop.

That is where professional Symbolism is headed. The power of perception has been demoralized. Nothing is real or authentic. The terrible *contredanses* of "correspondences," all nodding to each other. Eternal winking. Not a single clear word; only references and implications. The rose nods at the girl, the girl at the rose. Nobody wants to be himself. The epoch of Russian Poetry dominated by the Symbolists surrounding the journal, *The Scales,* was quite remarkable indeed. It developed an enormous structure that stood on clay feet and might best be defined as the epoch of pseudosymbolism. This should not be confused with the references to pseudoclassicism that denigrate the excellent poetry and fruitful style of Racine. Pseudoclassicism is a catchword attached by academic ignorance to a great style. Russian pseudosymbolism is really pseudosymbolism. Jourdan discovered in the maturity of his years that all his life he had been speaking prose. The Russian Symbolists discovered that very same prose—the primal figurative nature of the word. They put a stamp on all words, all images, designating them exclusively for liturgical use. This had very uncomfortable results —no passing through, no rising, no sitting down. Impossible to sit down at table for dinner, because it wasn't simply a table. Impossible to light a fire, because it might signify something that would make you unhappy.

Man was no longer master in his own house; it would turn out he was living in a church or in a sacred druidic grove. Man's domestic eye had no place to relax, nothing on which to rest. All creation was in revolt. The broom asked holiday, the cooking pot no longer wanted to cook, but demanded for itself an absolute significance (as if cooking were not an absolute significance). They had driven the master from his home and he no longer dared to enter there.[15]

15. Osip Mandelstam, "O prirode slova," *Sobranie sochinenii v trekh tomakh,* ed. Gleb Struve and Boris Filipoff, 2d ed. (Washington, D.C., 1967–1971), 2:254–55. Mandelstam takes as epigraph for this article a quotation from Gumilev's poem, "The Word," including the lines quoted above. The passage must not, of course, be construed as an argument for literalism; Mandelstam thought of himself as a "true" Symbolist. The translation of this extract is my own.

For Russian Modernism, 1909 was a crisis year. The Symbolists quarreled among themselves. Valery Briusov wrote that Symbolism, after having emancipated Russian literature from the claims of the social and the political, the utilitarian-reformist-revolutionary criteria that had dominated intelligentsia taste from the 1860s to the 1890s, now stood in danger of subordinating art to religion.[16] Two camps formed among the Symbolists: one, religious and mystical, which included in their different ways Viacheslav Ivanov, Andrei Biely, Fyodor Sologub; the other, esthetic, or moral-esthetic, consisting of Briusov and Konstantin Bal'mont. Blok, the greatest of them, was unhappy in either camp. A very strong reaction set in against the tendency toward vagueness, private language, intellectual isolation.

A minor poet and brilliant editor, Sergey Makovsky, founded the journal *Apollo,* which counterbalanced and then supplanted the Symbolist journal, *The Scales*. There Gumilev's "Letters on Russian Poetry" appeared, following a kind of proclamation by Mikhail Kuzmin, "On Beautiful Clarity." The current ran against obscurity, against private meaning, against the cult-significance of the poet and poetry; in favor of common speech, clear conventional form, and a more down-to-earth craftsmanly attitude. Gumilev founded the first Guild of Poets (the second he founded after his return to Russia in 1918) and tried to teach the techniques of verse.

Two of his students were far greater poets than he—Anna Akhmatova and Osip Mandelstam: Akhmatova, supreme mistress of the verbal gesture, poetess of tragic love, who became, in her old age, the poetess, too, of endurance and survival; Mandelstam, a kind of modern Ovid, poet of metamorphoses, the voice of eros as well as of civilization in an age of massive political tyranny and poetic vulgarization that, though he was no wolf and could be killed only by one of his peers, leaped for his throat like a wolfhound.[17] Personally Akhmatova had had painfully to liberate herself from Gumilev. Mandelstam's gifts were altogether superior, yet at no point had these talents ever come together in the kind of explicitness that Gumilev advocated. Deep ironist and visionary, Mandelstam could never even be imagined in a military pose

16. V. Briusov, quoted by H. W. Chalsma in *Russian Acmeism,* p. 14: "Is it possible that after art has been forced to serve science and society, it will now be forced to serve religion! At long last, give it its freedom. . . ." Gumilev did not hesitate to credit the Symbolists with having raised the cultural level of Russian literature after the provincialism and narrow utilitarianism of the 1880s.

17. "This wolfhound age leaps for my throat / Though I am not of wolf-blood," Osip Mandelstam in "For thunderous valor of days to come," *Sobranie sochinenii,* ed. Gleb Struve and Boris Filipoff (Munich, 1967), 1:162.

or adolescent-heroic gesture. Yet Mandelstam and Akhmatova, too, remained loyal to Gumilev as a teacher. Mandelstam on the entire subject of literary "schools" was skeptical and disparaging. But like Tsarskoe Selo where it originated, Acmeism, he said, was a "yearning for world culture." [18]

ACMEISM was sometimes called Adamism by Gumilev and his disciples. Thus, a kind of alpha and omega: a primal beginning and a final ripeness. Adam was the first poet, the name-giver, and as one who worshipped the living word it was natural for Gumilev to identify with Adam. And also with the primal and the primitive in general; with Africa; with its energy; and the setting it provided for the bringing into a fullness of being the "basic" human impulses—poetry, battle, kingly rule, erotic passion. And the contention of impulses, each wrought to its uttermost—poet and warrior, priest and king, body and soul; the primitive drama, and possibly also the primal scene.[19]

Gumilev identifies himself with Adam both before and after the fall. In a number of his early poems there are traces of infatuation with "my friend Lucifer," a haunting diabolism and a sense of doom: "Lucifer my friend gave me five horses" (see "A Ballad," p. 29). They are the five senses. In a much later poem, Gumilev details the painful formation of a "Sixth Sense" (see p. 116). In the early ballad quoted above, he quite explicitly names that sense:

> And laughing, mocking, contemptuous,
> Lucifer threw open the gates of darkness: for me.
> And he gave me a sixth horse,
> and the horse was named Despair.

Despair, martyrdom, suicide, these are themes in Gumilev that appear almost inevitably in connection with a shadowy female presence, a "moon-girl," or a "bird-girl"; often there is a flame or a "pillar of fire," always there is a sense of haunting unattainability, erotic frustration: "and there I saw a girl, and her face was sad (see p. 29)." Perhaps like Pushkin's Tsarskoe Selo statue she contemplates her "shattered urn." Perhaps another name for the shattered urn is incest, the prerogative (or fate) of aristocracy.[20]

18. Anna Akhmatova, "Mandelstam," *Vozdushnye puti,* no. 4 (1965), pp. 23–43. The remark is also quoted by Nadezhda Mandelstam in her memoir, *Hope Against Hope* (New York, 1970), p. 262.

19. The motifs of his African stories very much resemble those in his other work. See especially "Princess Zara," pp. 158–62. It seems likely that Gumilev's African journeys coincided with troubled times in his relations with women.

20. Pragmatically speaking, incest is a problem associated with the isolation of the upper classes and the overcrowding of the lower. I do not, of course, mean literally to accuse

In Gumilev's play, *Gondla,* the incest theme becomes very explicit. The play is set in Iceland of the eighth century. The hero, Gondla, is a poet, the son of an Irish skald, doomed to martyrdom in pagan Iceland. Unlike the hero of *The Poisoned Tunic,* also a poet but beautiful and powerful in body, Gondla is a hunchback and ineffectual against the Icelandic warriors. Yet his soul has as its proper emblem the swan, and he is a Christian, as opposed to his Icelandic antagonists, who are people of the wolf, and pagans. Gondla falls in love with and marries his half sister in whom the swan and the wolf contend. For the Christian Gondla, incestuous love becomes the very fabric of his doom. In the end, he dies a martyr's death. On the basis of his death, a new civilization is founded.[21]

In his neoclassical drama, *The Poisoned Tunic* (see p. 179), Gumilev's playwrighting suggests the symmetry of the art of mosaic. The action is set in sixth-century Byzantium. There is much about the play that is adolescent in taste and tone; except for the craftsmanship and the characterization of Zoe, it is reminiscent, say, of James Elroy Flecker's *Hassan* or the overblown poetic dramas of Edmond Rostand. Yet the craftsmanship—the "difficulty"—seems not altogether misapplied.

There are two Adams—both noble and eloquent: one, the king of Trapezond; the other, the pagan Arab poet, Imru-al-Kaish.[22] Both are corrupted and destroyed by the city, symbolized by Theodora, the universal whore. Both fall in love with Theodora's stepdaughter, Zoe, so desirable in her innocence amidst the corrupt city as to be inevitably destructive. Overtly there is no question of incest, and even Zoe's age (she is thirteen) is referred to the customs of time and place. Yet Imru

Gumilev of incestuous relations either with his mother or with the cousin his sister-in-law says was his abiding love. I am more interested in the sublimated incestuous motifs that appear so frequently in his poems. It is interesting, however, that when Gumilev's father died in 1910, Nikolai Stepanovich upset his mother by moving immediately into his father's study and in general taking over. In April of that year he married Akhmatova. Before the year was out, he was off to Abyssinia hunting elephants in the jungle and leopards in the mountains (A. A. Gumileva, "Nikolai Stepanovich Gumilev," pp. 114–15).

21. Gumilev, *Sobranie sochinenii,* 3:39–94. Wolf and swan: not only pagan and Christian, but also male and female. Gondla's half sister, in addition to the "moon-girl," suggests sexual ambiguity. "The city has a double nature. The genius of the city is secret—a city is a secret, founded or hidden, *ab urbe condita*—and what is secret about it is its sex: *sive mas, sive femina,* whether it is male or female . . ." (Norman O. Brown, "Roma—Amor," paper presented to the American Historical Association, December 1967).

22. Imru-al-Kaish was a historical figure. The king of Trapezond is entirely Gumilev's conception. Gumilev was fascinated by Rome, which he urged his brother and sister-in-law to visit. He was especially impressed with Saint Peter's and "the wolf-bitch with bloody jaws on her white, white column . . ." (A. A. Gumileva, "Nikolai Stepanovich Gumilev," p. 117).

has sworn a warrior's vow to remain chaste until the accomplishment of his mission; and Zoe has been officially betrothed to the king of Trapezond, who is inspired at first also by a kind of paternal attitude towards Imru. Zoe's seduction by Imru impels Trapezond to suicide and results in the agonized death of Imru in a poisoned tunic prepared by Justinian. The vows broken are not without analogy to the incest taboo. In the end, the seemingly innocent Zoe, like her whorish stepmother, is completely identified with the city of her birth and she is compared in her impact on men to the tunic. (Curiously enough, the play was a product of Gumilev's Parisian love of 1917 with "Elena D.," to whom the poems of *The Dark-Blue Star* were written.)

Behind the figure of Eve there flickers the "moon-girl," Lilith, who haunts every love. Whether she tokens the lost innocence of the garden or a more drastic "fall" is far from clear.

> What I took from the serpent's nest,
> the serpent's nest in Kiev,
> was a witch, not a wife.[23]

In an earlier poem to Akhmatova (who was once sketched in her long-necked grace by Modigliani), Gumilev uses as an analogue for his wife's mysterious and ambiguous beauty the silent, ineffable movements of a giraffe (see p. 37):

> . . . far, far away, near Lake Chad
> a delicate giraffe grazes up and down.

One of Gumilev's late poems is called "Bird-Girl" (see p. 113). Written in a ballad form congenial to Gumilev, it has a distinctly Symbolist, indeed even Maeterlinckian, setting—the never-never land of Celtic mists and myths, where the Arthurian romances, and most particularly the tales of Merlin (son of a forest-virgin and the devil himself) and Vivien (the wellspring of life) and the crystal cave, have their origin. Yet it is too explicit to be a Symbolist poem. Indeed, the explicitness of the sexual encounter between the shepherd and the bird-girl brings the poem to the edge of the absurd. Nevertheless, at that far edge of taste and credibility, the absurd blends with a vision of horror and solitude that is genuinely haunting.

The "happy shepherd" piping his affirmation of life is confronted by the beautiful but melancholy bird-girl in the never-never land of Broseliana. Everything about her hints at tormented complexities,

---

23. "From the Serpent's Nest," see p. 49. This poem is unusually playful for Gumilev, not often given to humor. It has much charm.

> . . . a flame-red
> bird with a tiny girl's head.
>
> It sang, then stopped, then sang,
> then stopped, like a baby crying in its sleep.
> Its lazy black eyes reminded him
> of Indian slaves.

She bewails her solitude:

> "Nowhere on the green earth,
> nowhere, is there another
>
> "Like me. . . ."

And she seems almost to reproach the shepherd for his normalcy:

> "You're young. You'll marry,
> you'll father children,"

while she promises to haunt even his descendants with the vision of her suffering beauty:

> "and then the Bird-girl
> will be remembered. . . ."

She prophesies that she will give birth to a son, cursed with her own loneliness, and unable to relieve her solitude,

> ". . . for I
> must die for him to be born.
>
> . . . .
>
> "He'll fly here, there,
> he'll sit in these elms,
> he'll call to his mate,
> and his mate will be dead."

But the bird-girl dies immediately after her encounter with the shepherd—her death is part of the encounter—and no son is born. Except, of course, that the shepherd becomes her son as well as her mate. In taking him as her lover, she makes him also her heir:

> The shepherd pipes funeral songs
> over her body.
>
> Twilight.
> Gray mist.

> He drives his flock home,
> away from Broseliana.

THE poems about destiny and fate in the last two volumes of Gumilev's poetry, *Bonfire* and *Pillar of Fire,* display a depth and a resonance beyond his earlier poems. "The Muzhik" (see p. 98) is a poem about Rasputin; at the same time it is a vision of the half-pagan Russian peasants marching from the damp, dark places of the primitive Russian forests against the fragile cross hung over Saint Isaac's and the Kazan Cathedral in Petrograd to overwhelm the rudiments of urban civilization, to claim back their own. "A Workman" (see p. 97) is a curious poem of praise to the artisan who will forge the bullet that will kill Gumilev:

> . . . And this was done by the small
> old man in the faded grey blouse.

The worker, who is calm and submissive to fate as Gumilev is, performs his job, stubbornly acts out his anonymous role in the fated event that is to be Gumilev's death.

In "Primal Memories" (see p. 96) Gumilev speaks out against the teeming energy of Africa, and in favor of the quiescence of India, the calm and detachment of oriental philosophy, which also intimates an analogue with his approaching death:

> And when will I finally end
> this dream, and be myself—
> a humble Indian dozing
> in the sacred twilight, along some quiet river?

The greatest of these poems is called "The Lost Tram" (see p. 105). The scene is immediately set in an urban landscape, an unfamiliar street in Petrograd, through which sound ominous rumblings:

> . . . crows
> croaking, then the sound of a lute
> and thunder crawling slow
> from a distance. . . .

If Lermontov, whom Gumilev seems so much to resemble, describes his cosmic destiny as setting out alone along a highroad, Gumilev describes his as leaping on a tram from an unfamiliar street to an unknown destination: cheap, modern transportation; democratic (anybody can ride; everybody does), convenient (it goes right by; you just have to jump on) and commonplace—yet, powerful, ineluctable, and mysterious:

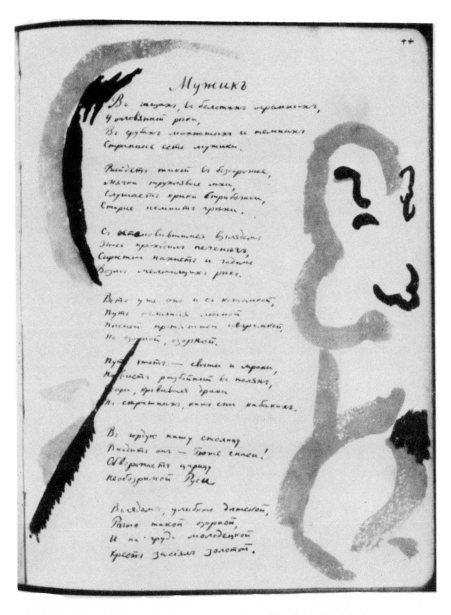

The first page of the original manuscript of "The Muzhik,"
illustrated by M. F. Larionov in his Paris album. From
Gumilev, *Sobranie sochinenii,* 2:12 (private collection of
Gleb Struve).

> . . . a trail
> of fire streaking like sunrays.

> Rushing like a storm with dark wings. . . .

The oncoming tram and the oncoming storm are analogous.

Although on rails, "the tram blundered and was lost." The passenger repeats the recurrent nightmare of all those who have used the public transport of a large metropolitan city: the conductor doesn't hear, the doors won't open, the crowd refuses to give way; he is caught. The tram takes him from Petersburg to all the places of his life, and back to Petersburg. He is haunted by the brief glimpse of a blind beggar in Beirut. The beggar is dead and gone. As in a death-wish dream, the appearance of a person known to be dead presages the dreamer's own wished-for death. The beggar has "knowing eyes."

The tram is lost in time as well as space. Fragments of the past, present, future flash by.

The station where they sell tickets for "the India of the Spirit" ("Passage, O my soul, to India . . .")—the spiritual direction in which Gumilev, under the impact of his war experiences, seemed to have been moving—that, too, flashes by. Next, a sign marked Grocer, a greengrocer actually; in Russian, simply the adjective "green." What takes place there, however, is a bloodying, not a greening. It is the Revolution, lopping off heads. The passenger sees his own head slopped into a box of heads.

The butcher has a head like an udder. The repulsive image contributes to the generally apocalyptic hints and allusions, a suggestion of the "dragon red and hidden harlot," and also the wolf-bitch, mother of cities, that suckled Romulus and Remus.[24]

Then the tram passes a typical old-fashioned Russian house, unpainted wood, with a wooden fence:

> Mashenka: you lived here, and sang,
> and wove me a rug, and promised
> to marry me . . .

Gumilev's sister-in-law, A. A. Gumileva, has written in a recent memoir of Gumilev's early love for his cousin, Masha Kuz'mina-Karavaeva.

24. See note 23. "The sphinx, the she-wolf, the dragon red and hidden harlot, the Great City, is a woman with a penis—the prick (*acus*) of the Mother of the Gods on which the safety of Rome depended . . . the horn of the beast of the woman of the Apocalypse. A phallic mother, a female hidden in a male, 'a Dragon red and hidden Harlot,' which Blake said was the same religion hid on war . . ." (Norman O. Brown, "Roma—Amor." See also Brown's *Love's Body* [New York, 1966], pp. 63, 75).

Whether or not she was, as Gumilev's sister-in-law claims, his only true love, "Mashenka" seems to be addressed to her.[25] She is also the girl of the gypsy songs and the love-ballads, the old-fashioned Russian girl, Russia herself.[26] The passenger speaks of himself as having been betrothed to her, but having heard her moan

> . . . when I powdered
> my hair to present myself
> to the Empress. I never
> saw you again.

Powdered hair and presentation to the Empress suggests the eighteenth-century Russian nobility, the *dvorianstvo,* which enjoyed its golden age in the service of Catherine II of German origin; enlightened correspondent of Grimm, Diderot, and Voltaire; playwright and editor of society journals; at whose court the nobility became Europeanized and, without altogether losing its ideals of service or of a civilizing mission, alienated from its Russian roots ("I never saw you again"). It was under the Empresses Elizabeth and Catherine that Petersburg took on its most characteristic aspects—the rococo palaces, the summer houses, the cleverly planned vistas and perspectives. But Catherine, the would-be *philosophe* who ornamented Petersburg, bought Diderot's library, and spoke high-mindedly of the law, also extended serfdom, ruthlessly suppressed the Pugachev uprising, and sent the intellectuals Novikov and Radishchev off to exile. As during her reign, the melancholy proximity and inevitable bond between civilization and repressive power suffuses Gumilev's poem.

Falconet's equestrian statue of Peter the Great catches the passenger's eye—"an iron glove and two hooves . . ." It is the Bronze Horseman, celebrated by Pushkin in his poem of that title. Unlike Pushkin's poor clerk, Evgeny, the central figure of that poem, the passenger does not rebel against the imperious gesture of the statue's outstretched hand. And the statue remains on its pedestal as the tram goes by. And then, another Petersburg landmark comes into view, token of peace and reconciliation, the dome of Saint Isaac's Cathedral:

> let them sing for Mashenka
> and mourn for me.

25. A. A. Gumileva, "Nikolai Stepanovich Gumilev," pp. 114–16. Gleb Struve is highly skeptical of Gumileva's reading a lifelong obsession into Gumilev's affection for his cousin (Gumilev, *Sobranie sochinenii,* 1:viii).

26. This is expounded at somewhat greater length in the very interesting master's thesis by Wladislaw Krasnow, "Gumilev's Late Poetry," University of Washington, 1968.

How can I breathe? It hurts
to live. My heart tears
itself. Mashenka, I never knew
how much love and sorrow we can bear.

If Blok's "The Twelve" was the poem of the Revolution, Gumilev's
"Lost Tram" becomes the poem of Saint Petersburg, Imperial City and
monument to civilization. Ironically, the one image in the poem that
seems forced is that likening Saint Isaac's dome to "God's true hand,"
for the opulent and oppressive Imperial spirit is elegantly embodied in
the gold and marble of Nicholas's cathedral—Nicholas I, the persecutor
of Pushkin—and by the cathedral itself one is reminded rather of "Religion hid in War," as in Blake's "Milton," than of peace and understanding.[27]

Gumilev once wrote that the essence of a poem was "sensuality re-
pressed."[28] So Freud wrote of civilization. The tram is now an archaic
vehicle, and Petersburg is Leningrad; but somehow Gumilev's poem,
like the discontent of our civilization, hovers in the air like a cry.

27. Brown, *Love's Body*, p. 63.
28. The Russian phrase is *podavlennaia chuvstvennost'*, which Chalsma translates as
"suppressed sensuality" in *Russian Acmeism*, p. 84. See Gumilev, "Zhizn' stikha," *So-
brani sochinenii*, 4:157. Gumilev advocated, as Chalsma put it, "the subjection of all
feeling to the acid test of pure form" (p. 84). This is, of course, an aspect of his Puri-
tanical fetishism of the difficult.

Poetry

From *Romantic Flowers* (1903–1907)

A Ballad

Lucifer my friend gave me five horses
and one gold ruby ring,
for me to go down, down into the ground,
for me to see the sky's young face.

My horses beat their hooves, snorted, begged
to gallop like birds all over the earth,
and I believed the sun's light burned for me,
glowing like my ruby gold ring.

Oh the star-filled nights, oh the flame-filled days
I roamed the earth, roamed the earth all over,
laughing at my wild horses
and the light from my gold ring.

And the heights of consciousness lie covered with madness, and with
    snow,
but my whip whistled as I beat my horses on
and up the heights of consciousness they ran
and there I saw a girl, and her face was sad,

And music rang in her quiet voice,
and questions turned to answers in her strange eyes,
and I gave her my ring, this moon-girl,
for the shifting shades of her careless hair.

And laughing, mocking, contemptuous,
Lucifer threw open the gates of darkness: for me.
And he gave me a sixth horse,
and the horse was named Despair.

Recollection

Out at sea, at noon,
sparks dance and the sun glows,
and the bird that's flown too far
sobs with speechless eyes.

The green sea lured her out,
covered her eyes with mist,
and now she must fly and fly
to the end, high over the silent sea.

Whimsical whirlwinds tug her,
and trying to turn back is worthless,
her heavy white wings
will never bring her home.

And when I saw your eyes,
sad summer lightning hidden inside them,
I saw that same horror,
the exhausted bird's same silent reproach.

Thoughts

They have crowded around me—why?—like thieves
in the dark, in the quiet suburban dark.
Like sinister hawks, like sullen hawks,
they have come for some cruel vengeance.

Hope left. Dreams ran.
Anxiety pried open my eyes
and as though on a ghostly slate
I read my words, my deeds, my plans.

Because I watched them sailing
to victories, my eyes calm—
Because I touched sinless lips
with burning lips—

Because these hands, these fingers,
are frail, have never known a plough—
Because songs, those everlasting gypsies,
have come to me only in pain, ringing, dark—

For all of this the time of vengeance has come.
Blind men will pull down the lying, delicate temple,
and thoughts, thieves in the suburban peace,
will strangle me in the darkness, like a beggar.

The Cross

Card after card lied to me, lied and lied,
and even wine no longer helped.
Cold March stars hung pale,
anxious, outside the window.

Coldly mad, in a crazy passion,
I felt the game was a dream.
"I bet everything in the bank, all of it!" I shouted.
And I lost.

I left. Dawn shadows
moved gently, lovingly over the delicate snow.
I can't remember how, but I fell
on my knees, my gold cross pressed to my lips:

"Oh to be free, to be pure, like the sky, like the stars,
to accept your staff, oh Sister Poverty,
to wander, to beg my bread,
commanding men's souls with this sacred cross!"

Another moment—and then everyone in that noisy,
laughing hall shrank back, frightened,
as I stalked insanely through the room
and bet my cross on the next card.

The Rat

The icon candle flickers, small,
the half-dark nursery is horribly quiet.
The frightened child
hides in the pink lace bed.

What's that? The house spirit coughing?
He lives there, he's little, he's bald . . .
Agh! A vicious rat creeps slowly
from behind the wardrobe.

It waves its prickly whiskers
in the red glow of the icon,
wondering if the little child is in the little bed,
the small girl with large, large eyes.

"Momma! Momma!"—But momma has company,
and nurse Vasilisa's laughing in the kitchen,
and the rat's small red eyes
are burning happily, like coal.

Horrible to wait, more horrible to leave the bed.
Oh bright-winged angel, where are you? where?
Oh Angel, come quick, come quick,
save me from the rat, have mercy on me!

The Choice

He who builds the tower will fall.
He will fall straight down, terribly,
and at the deep bottom of the world's well
he will curse himself for his madness.

He who pulls the tower down will be crushed,
flattened by stone shards;
and left to lie there, by All-Seeing God,
he will howl his torment.

And he who went into the caverns of night,
and he who went to the backwaters of a quiet river,
will suddenly confront the awful eyes
of the bloodthirsty panther.

Fate is inescapable,
everyone on earth has his own destiny.
But hush! The one incomparable right
is to choose your death for yourself.

Beyond the Grave

There's a secret cavern, deep in the earth,
filled with stately tombs,
Lucifer's fiery dreams.
Beautiful whores slink between them.

Whether you die proud or ashamed
a gloomy old man, a bony old man,
a boring, sluggish workman—Death—
will come and stare at you imperiously.

He'll carry you down corridors,
he'll carry you from tower to tower.
Your eyes glassy, bulging, you'll understand
that this is the way the dream unfolds.

And then, dropped into your tomb,
you'll start to dream of heaven's temple,
and you'll suddenly see
a whore with pearly-sharp teeth.

How sweetly she'll press you to her,
kissing you with infinite spite.
You can't move. You can't scream.
That's all there is. Forever and forever.

The Founders

Romulus and Remus went up a hill,
a wild and silent hill.
Said Romulus, "Here there'll be a city."
Said Remus, "A city like the sun."

Said Romulus, "We found our ancient honor
by grace of the stars."
Said Remus, "The past is dead,
let it be forgotten. Consider the future."

Said Romulus, "Here we'll put the circus,
and here our house, open to everyone."
Said Remus, "But the tombs, the tombs
must be nearer the house."

The Giraffe

You are sadder, today: I can see.
And your arms, wrapped around your knees, are thinner.
But listen: far far away, near Lake Chad,
a delicate giraffe grazes up and down.

He is blessed with sinuous beauty and with happiness,
and his hide is stamped with a magic design
that only the moon dares to challenge,
splitting, rocking white on the waters of wide lakes.

From far off he seems like colored sails on a ship,
he runs like a smooth-flying gay-flying bird.
When he hides in a marble cave, at sunset,
earth sees wonders, I know it does.

I know cheerful stories of mysterious lands,
about lovely black girls, about passionate young chiefs,
but you have breathed too much heavy fog,
you refuse to believe in anything but rain.

And how shall I tell you about tropical gardens,
about slender palms, about the perfume of unimaginable grasses . . .
You're crying? Listen . . . far far away, near Lake Chad,
a delicate giraffe grazes up and down.

From *Pearls* (1907–1910)

Descendants of Cain

He told us no lies, that harsh spirit with sad
eyes and the morning star's name:
he said, "Don't worry about Heaven's vengeance;
eat of the fruit and be like gods."

Young men can go anywhere, now,
old men can do anything,
and girls have
amber fruit and unicorns white as snow.

But why do our knees go weak,
why do we feel forgotten by Someone,
why do we understand the horror of the ancient temptation

When someone's hand, by accident
and only for a moment, knots
two sticks, two blades of grass, two poles, and shapes a cross?

Don Juan

I have a simple, arrogant dream:
I will lift the oar, leap into the stirrup,
and cheat slow time,
I will kiss only new lips.

And when I am old I will receive Christ,
turn down my eyes, sprinkle ashes on my head,
and let the glorious weight of salvation
hang, an iron cross, on my chest.

And when I break away from the orgy,
like a sleepwalker waking, pale and frightened,
to the sound of his silent feet,

Then, only then I remember that I am a superfluous
atom, never father to a woman's child,
never any man's brother.

The Gates of Paradise

The eternal entrance to Heaven is not
locked with seven diamond seals;
it does not glitter, no one is tempted,
and so no one knows it.

It's only stones and moss, that's all,
a door in an old, abandoned wall.
A beggar stands there, like an uninvited guest,
stands with keys at his belt.

Hussars and knights ride by,
trumpets howling, silver clanking,
without a look at the doorman,
Peter, the shining apostle.

They all dream, "There, at God's Tomb,
we will see the doors of Paradise open for us,
there at the foot of Mount Tabor,
there the promised hour will ring."

The slow monster winds by,
howling, loud,
and Peter in his beggar's
rags stands miserable, pale.

Prayer

Ferocious sun, malevolent sun,
insane face
of God, walking out in space,

Sun, burn away the present
for the sake
of the future, but spare the past!

At the Stern Temple

At the stern temple
he knelt to the Madonna's statue
and swore eternal truth
to the lady with faithful eyes.

And he forgot his secret marriage,
and spread his love like a feast.
One night he was stabbed in a duel
and came to Heaven's doors—

But the Madonna thundered,
"In my temple you swore
eternal truth
to the lady with faithful eyes.

"Leave! The King of Heaven does not reap
your kind of harvest.
Breakers of oaths
die, strangers to God."

Sad and stubborn
he fell at Her feet:
"I have yet to meet
the lady with faithful eyes."

A Quiet, Dull Place

The sun went down in the west
beyond the promised fields,
and this quiet, dull place
turned dark-blue, fragrant.

The reeds shook faintly,
a bat flew by,
a fish splashed in the still pond . . .
And those who have a home
started home, toward
blue shutters, toward
ancient armchairs, toward
round tea tables.

Only I stayed outside,
watching this quiet, dull place
where by daylight it is delight to swim,
where at night it is delight to weep,
because, Lord, it is You I love.

From *Foreign Sky* (1910–1912)

From the Serpent's Nest

What I took from the serpent's nest,
the serpent's nest in Kiev,
was a witch, not a wife.
I wanted a girl for the fun of it,
some high-powered fun girl,
some singing songbird.

Call her: she makes a face.
Hug her: she fights back.
The moon shines, she moans,
and stares, goes limp
like a mourner at a grave
—and wants to drown

Herself. I try to tell her: look,
a good Christian like me
shouldn't mess with you.
Why not go away, you and your moaning,
down to the Dnieper whirlpools,
over to wild Bald Mountain.

Nothing, not a word. She sits by herself,
feeling lousy,
and I feel sorry for her
guilt, she's like a bird I
shot, a birch tree I dug out,
a birch tree leaning over bewitched ground.

The Urchin

I'll walk along the tracks,
thinking, following
the thread of the running rails
across the yellow sky, the scarlet sky.

I'll go to the gloomy
station, shivering—
if the watchmen don't shout
and chase me off.

And later, determined to remember,
I'll think—again, again—
of the beautiful lady, and how she looked up,
quickly, as she got into the train.

Proud, distant:
Why should she care if I love her?
But when will I ever see
another lady with eyes so blue!

I'll tell my friend,
I'll tease him, a little,
when evening spreads smoke
across the meadow.

And with an ugly smile
he'll say, "You see?
You read all kinds of junk
and you start to talk like that."

Love

Arrogant as a boy, the lyric
poet came in, did not knock,
said only that I was now
to love only him. Only him.

With a scowl he slammed
my book shut, stamped
his patent leather shoe and
murmured, "How dull."

The nerve, to be perfumed like that!
The gall, to stand fiddling with his rings!
Incredible, how he spilled flowers
across my desk, my bed!

I strode out of the house, peeved,
but he would not let me go,
he walked alongside, banging his crazy
cane on the pavement.

And now I've gone insane.
I don't dare go home,
I keep talking about *him,* and
I use his shameless language.

To a Girl

I don't care for the indolence
in your crossed arms,
their calm modesty,
their shy fright.

You could have been written by Turgenev:
haughty, delicate, pure,
reeking of autumn that never
roars down the lane, where leaves whirl.

Everything you believe
is measured, first, is rational, balanced;
before you leave the house
you find your way on a map.

You know nothing, nothing! of the hunter
who climbs a bare straight cliff
and torn with joy, blessed with anguish,
shoots an arrow up at the sun.

Fragment

Christ said, "Blessèd are the poor;
the blind, the lame, the beggars are fortunate;
for I will take them to my home above the stars,
I will make them Knights of Heaven,
they will be the most glorified of the glorified . . ."
All right, suppose it's true: all right! But
what about the others
whose thoughts we breathe by, whose thoughts
we live, whose very names are trumpet-calls?
How will they atone for greatness,
what will the turning balance-wheel deal out to them?
Is Beatrice already a whore, in Heaven,
Goethe a deaf-mute beggar,
Byron an organ-grinder's monkey . . . oh, *merde, merde!*

The Eternal

In a tunnel of locked days
where even the sky presses painfully
I can see centuries, I live in minutes,
but I wait for the Sabbath of Sabbaths:

The end of anxiety, the end of success, the end
to my soul's blind wandering . . .
Oh time when I too will open my eyes
and know, oh hurry!

I will have a new soul,
everything exciting will be in it.
I will bless the golden road
stretching from worm to sun.

And he who walked at my side
in thunder and in silence,
who frowned at my delight,
who smiled at my sin,

Who taught me peace, who taught me war,
taught me earth's ancient wisdom—
he will drop his staff, and turn,
and say, simply, "Here, we've arrived."

From *Tent* (1907–1913)

Prelude to *Tent*

Of you, Africa, deafened by howling
and the clatter of hooves, surrounded by fire and smoke,
it is of you they speak in Heaven,
seraphim whispering your name.

And opening your Gospel,
the story of your terrible, your wonderful life,
they think of the fumbling new angel
ordered, O reckless one, to watch over you.

You, hanging like a great pear
on the ancient tree of Eurasia,
listen to what you've done, what you've dreamed,
the song of your beast-like soul.

Blood-linked to you, I will tell
of chiefs in leopard skins
leading mobs of sullen soldiers through dark forests,
and to victory;

Of villages with ancient idols
laughing with evil lips,
and lions stalking above villages,
clanging their tails on their ribs.

Only, give me a smooth road
there where no man has walked,
let that unknown black river
flow with my name.

And—a final favor,
before I go to the holy places—
let me die under that same sycamore
where Mary rested with Christ.

The Sahara

All deserts are one tribe, from the beginning
of time, but Arabia, Syria, Gobi—
they're only ripples of the vast Sahara
wave that roared its satanic spite.

The Red Sea heaves, and the Persian Gulf,
and Pamir stands thick with snow,
but Sahara's sand-floods
run straight to green Siberia.

Not in dense forests, not on huge oceans,
but only in the desert, only the desert,
do you need no other men, meet no others,
and love only sun and wind.

The sun bends from its blue heights,
bends down its young girl's face,
and the golden dunes
are like rivers of spilled sun.

Porphyry palaces in the cliffs, and purple towers,
and palms and fountains on guard:
sun-painted mirages
on glassy air-mirrors.

And at evening, violet shadows
painted in the sand, under
cliffs and under bushes, painted
as if on a smooth gold board.

And at a sign from the sky
desert music rings out;
limestone, bursting with flames, spills
and scatters into dark-red dust.

Rock peaks gleam, and dark between them,
below them, dry stone rivers
sleep. The Sahara: only a wave-tossed
stormy sea?

Look closer: the eternal glory of sand
reflects celestial flames:

the sky—where clouds curl into sleep,
where rainbows drift: the Sahara is like the sky.

Wind, wild wind, is the second lord
of the desert, rushing
like an Indian stallion down
ravines and over high hills—

And sand rings and sings, and climbs to its feet,
knowing its master.
The air darkens, the sun's eye narrows
like a pomegranate center.

Dust whirlwinds swell
like ancient, monstrous palm trees,
bend, sway, move in the darkness
as if never intending to fall,

Wandering till the end of time,
more and more awesome,
serpent heads disappear in clouds,
terrible grey snake-heads.

Then one of them lags, falters,
falls in a heap of sand,
tripping on a camel
bellowing in terror.

And like new mountains they all lie down
on the flat, smooth plain,
and the hot, dry desert wind blows
to the sea, seeding trouble, stupefying.

And a caravan mills around, the guide
poking the sand with his stick, frightened,
hunting a once-familiar spring
but not finding it.

And horses neigh, in green oases,
and Himalayan nard scents the air
under palm trees—islands as rare in an ocean
of fire as spots on a black leopard.

But howling, too, deafening howls
as spears glitter and burnooses blow—
for the Tibbusi to the east
hate the Tuaregs to the west.

And as they fight for a palm grove,
or a camel, or a slave girl,
sand sweeps in and covers
Tibesti, covers Murzuk, covers Gadames—

Desert winds respect
nothing, pull down
walls, bury gardens, poison
pools with snow-white salt.

And perhaps, in a hundred, two hundred
years, wild packs of sand-wolves
from the burning young Sahara
will rush at our old, green world,

Fill the Mediterranean,
fill Paris, and Moscow, fill Athens—
and we, bedouins on camels,
will believe in heavenly fires.

And then, in the end, when ships
from Mars dock on earth
all they'll see is an ocean of gold,
all, and they'll call it: Sahara.

Dahomey

And the king declared to his general, "Mighty one,
you're as tall as an elephant in our forests,
but not as tall as the triumphant heap
of heads you've cut off.

"And your courage, O well-tested warrior,
is endless, but so is my kindness.
Observe the sun above the sea: go! You deserve
to serve my golden father."

Drums pounded, tambourines clicked,
people wailed,
Amazon soldiers moaned long songs, and blowing horns
rolled out across the sea.

Silently the general bowed
to the king, leaped from the cliff, down to the whirling
water, and drowned in water but seemed
to drown in the gold glow of the setting sun.

Drums deafened him, howling deafened him,
salt spray blinded him,
and he was gone. And the king's face shone
like a black sun in hell.

Somaliland

I remember that night, that place,
the moon so low in the sky.

And I remember how I could not look away
from its golden path.

How light, there. And birds sing.
And flowers bloom above pools,

And there on the moon no one hears the roaring of lions
filling every crack in the earth,

And no prickly mimosa thorns clasp at you, there,
as you walk through the abyss of night!

That night, as shadows had just begun to crawl,
the Somalis came closer

And their chief, with his shaggy red hair,
pronounced my death,

His eyes lowered, but mocking
at how few men I had.

Tomorrow there will be war, nervous, merciless, boring,
war with a howling black crowd,

Tangles of bodies under camels' feet,
poisoned spears and arrows,

And I thought, painfully, that up on the moon, up on that moon
no enemy could crawl up at me.

At midnight I woke my people.
The ocean roared, behind the hill.

Sailors were dying, out at sea, and we earth-men
were waiting to die in the dark.

We left. The grass breathed
like a lion's sweaty hide,

And among the sacred black rocks
we saw piles of bones and skulls.

No more horrible place in all Africa: Somaliland.
No place more dismal,

Nowhere more white men speared in the darkness
alongside sandy wells

So Ogaden can count the killings
with the voices of hungry hyenas.

And when, before dawn, the moon bent down,
different, now, terrible and red,

I knew that, like a knight's shield,
she burned with eternal glory, but for heroes,

And I ordered the camels staked out and trusted
my soul to my gun.

The Red Sea

Greetings, Red Sea, shark soup,
Negro bath, sand cauldron!
Like stone cactus flowers
limestone, not moss, blooms on your cliffs.

Sea-monsters swept up by the tide lie dying
in anguish, out on your islands
in the burning sand: octopi,
tritons, swordfish.

From Africa dugouts swarm,
hunting pearls,
and from Arabia fast ships
swoop chasing them.

The Negroes they catch
are whipped in chains to the slave market,
but unlucky Arabs find peace
in your hot, dirty-red waves.

Like a teacher down aisles of playful children
steamboats pass through,
white water bubbling behind them,
red roses and ice on deck.

You can't disturb them: a hurricane can scream,
a wave rise like a crystal peak—
Lighting a cigar, the captain will sigh,
"*Mon Dieu,* how cool! What frightful heat!"

Gold flying fish, like grasshoppers, like dragonflies,
hum over the water;
sand curved like sickles against
flowering red and green reefs.

Transparent fire flashes in the air,
the sun glares down like a fairy-tale bird:
"Sea, oh Red Sea, you shine like a queen,
but you glow, you dazzle, you are blinding when darkness comes!"

Mist floats from the water, like tiny clouds,
and the shadows of black mermaids criss-cross in the waves!
And stars we've never heard of—like crosses, like axes—
blow into flames, in that garden in the sky.

And all your magic whorls
shimmer with Bengalese fire,
with sparks, with bright beams,
as if forging new stars in Heaven's face.

And then the moon drifts out,
and the wind rips by, covering the scent of forests,
and from Suez to Bab-el-Mandeb
you ring like an Aeolian harp.

Elephants come to your shore, bow
to roaring waves, worship
the failing moon, mirrored in your water
—but tremble at gleaming shark teeth.

And then you remember—a sea, only a sea—
how you obeyed God's Word
and tore your mighty tides apart
so Moses could walk and Pharaoh die.

From *The Quiver* (1912–1916)

The Sick Man

Only one thing torments my delirium:
how certain sharp lines go on for ever,
and a bell rings and rings and rings
like a clock marking off eternity.

Just so, after death,
eyes stare into darkness
(the agonized hope of resurrection)
trying to see familiar visions.

But there are no voices, there is no green grass
in that ocean of primordial blackness,
only cubes, angles, rhomboids,
and malicious ringing, that never stops.

Sleep: oh I want to be buried in sleep!
If only I could go away—a holiday of reconciliation—
to yellow sand and grey-haired seas
and count the big brown rocks.

Offensive

This country could have been paradise:
it's a den of fire.
We've been advancing for four days,
we've not eaten for four days.

In this strange, bright hour
we don't need earth's bread:
the Lord's Word
is better nourishment.

The blood-filled weeks
are blinding, insubstantial;
shrapnel bursts over my head,
knives fly faster than birds.

I shout, my voice wild,
"That's brass banging on brass!"
I carry a Great Idea,
I cannot die, I cannot.

Like thunder hammering,
like angry sea-waves,
Russia's golden heart
beats steadily in my chest.

And how sweet to dress Victory,
like a girl, in ropes of pearls,
as you follow the enemy's
smoke-covered retreating tracks.

The Cathedral at Padua

Marvellous, and sad—yes, that's what this temple
is—a joy, a temptation, a threat.
Eyes exhausted with desire
burn in the slits of confessional windows.

The organ melody rises, falls,
then swells fuller and more terrible,
like blood in dark church-granite veins
rioting in drunken mutiny.

I want to run out of these black arches,
away from purple velvet, away from languid martyrs,
their bare white bodies:
or temptation may possess my soul.

I need to sit at some remote old tavern, out
on the terrace, with a glass of wine—
there, right there, the stone wall has gone green,
turned green by the sea.

Hurry! One last try!
—but then, outside, you suddenly weaken—
Catholicism spreads its gothic towers,
like wings, in the blue sky.

The Sun of the Spirit

How could we walk in peace, before,
expecting no joy, no disaster,
not dreaming of battles, of flaming retreats,
or the roaring trumpet of victory?

How could we—but it's not too late,
the sun of the spirit bends down to us—
soothing, threatening, it pours
across our skies.

And our spirit flowers like a May rose,
tearing darkness apart like fire;
knowing nothing, blind, the body
obeys.

Out on the wild, beautiful plains,
in the quiet holiness of the deep forest,
the soul knows no torment
nor the will any difficulty.

It will be autumn, soon: I feel it.
The sun's work will be done
and people will pick golden fruit
from the tree of the spirit.

Evening

How thick, how wingless an evening!
A sunset like a cracked melon.

You almost want to shove
those limp clouds along.

Slow evenings like this,
coachmen whip their horses to a gallop,

Fishermen tear at the waves with their oars,
woodsmen chop like mad

At huge, bush-headed oaks . . .
and those who hold in their hands

The universal movement of all things, who keep
all rhythms, past, present, future,

They make poems with wings
and wake the universe from its sluggish sleep.

It Wasn't Living

It wasn't living, I wasted
half my life
—and then, Lord, You came to me
like this, in an impossible dream.

I see light on Mount Tabor
and my heart hurts
with love for the land and the sea
and the whole tree-dark dream of existence,

My heart hurts that
I wasn't Yours sooner,
that I was so tormented
by Your daughters' beauty.

But is love only a tiny red flower
with just a moment to bloom?
Is love only a tiny flame
so easy to snuff out?

Thinking these quiet, dismal thoughts
I'll manage to drag this life out
—But You think about the next one:
I've ruined one already.

From *To the Dark-Blue Star* (1918)

Did I Murder My Father

Did I murder my father, murder my mother,
in some other life?
Yes, oh immortal, eternal God, yes! or how
could I deserve this disgrace of suffering?

I lead a life as peaceful as death,
everything I do belongs to someone else, nothing
to me—except a languid, worthless,
distinctly platonic love . . .

Oh to run, to hide like a thief
—in Africa, as I hid before, to lie
beneath some royal sycamore
and never rise.

Darkness would wrap me in velvet,
the moon would dress me in silver,
and maybe the wind could forget
that, once, I worked in an office.

The Dark-Blue Star

Your tormenting, wonderful,
inevitable beauty
ripped me out of my thin,
miserable, puling life,

And I died. And I saw
a flame no one ever saw
before; my eyes went black, but I saw
a dark-blue star.

A song: soft, then loud, then soft:
body and soul melting:
that was your blood, ringing, speaking,
singing like a lyre.

And I knew a scent sweeter, heavier
with fire than anything on this earth—
a scent sweeter than lilies
in the gardens of Heaven.

And then this earth, this flat earth
came back, out of shimmering, brilliant depths—
you fluttered,
unforeseen, like a wounded bird,

Saying over and over, "I'm suffering."
—Yes, but what can I do when, at last,
I understand, smiling, that all you are
is a dark-blue star?

I Can't Forget

No, I can't ever forget
your child's mouth, your girl's glance,
bold—I dream of you,
I speak, I think of you—always—like rhythm.

I feel vast oceans
heaving as the moon yaws,
and whole galaxies, burning,
swinging as they have always swung, will always swing.

Oh, if you would stay with me—always—
smiling, sensible, as good as now,
I'd walk on those stars, and
I'd kiss the sun on its burning lips.

From *Bonfire* (1916–1918)

The Dream

My nightmare woke me, groaning
with the most intense pain.
My dream: that you loved someone else
and he had hurt you.

I ran out of bed
like a murderer from the guillotine,
and saw how the streetlights
shone dim, like animals' eyes.

Oh, no one, no one
could have wandered, that night,
so homeless, so alone, down dark streets
that were like the beds of dried-up rivers.

I'm standing in front of your door,
I've no other path,
but I know I can never
open that door.

He hurt you, I know;
I dreamed it, but the dream was true.
And all the same I lie dying
beneath your closed window.

She Who Scatters Stars

You're not always proud, aloof;
you don't always refuse me.

You come to me, sometimes,
quietly, quietly, quietly, like in a dream.

The hair above your forehead is heavy, full.
I'm never allowed to kiss it.

And your wide eyes
are lit by a magic moon.

My gentle friend, my merciless enemy,
your every step carries such blessing

That you might be walking along my heart,
scattering stars and flowers.

Where can you have found them?
Why do you glow so bright,

And having had you, for even a while,
why has earth so little left to love?

Canzonet I

How many of earth's oceans I've sailed, oceans
ancient, gay, foam-covered;
how many matchless nights and days
have gone guiding caravans across the steppes . . .

How we laughed, then,
my Muse and I, free . . .
Rhymes flew together like birds,
so many—I don't dare remember how many.

Only love is left, calling
like the strings of an angel's harp,
like a thin needle stabbing the heart
with Heaven's blue lights.

Only you are left. I've seen,
my eyes open, the night's sun,
and you are all I live for,
work for, fight for.

In this restless hell of mine—yes,
you are the pilgrims' Jerusalem.
I should mention your name
with a seraphim's tongue.

Canzonet 2

Your temple, Lord, is in Heaven,
but the earth is Your shelter, too.
Lime trees bloom in the forests,
and birds sing in the trees.

Like Your cathedral bells, spring
moves across the fields, gay,
and flying on a dream's wings
angels come to us, in spring.

If I speak the truth, Lord,
if I sing Your song,
let me have a sign; Lord, give me
a sign that I've known Your will.

Come, an Invisible Light,
to her who, now, sits sad,
and answer dazzling answers
to everything she asks.

You know, better than birds' singing,
better for the soul than Heaven's trumpets,
is the faint trembling of beloved eyes
And a smile on beloved lips.

Canzonet 3

How quiet Nature has gone!
All eyes, all ears.
Our spirit leans, leans
toward that final, awful freedom.

And earth will forget how soldiers
hurt her, how merchants sinned,
and Druids will teach on green hills
as once, once before they taught.

And poets will lead hearts on high,
as once, once before,
as angels point shooting stars
toward unseen targets.

And I will cry, "Where are you, woman
born of fire?
My eyes are unchanged,
my song is unchanged,

"I remain your beauty's servant,
my power is still your power,
and real happiness, final
happiness, is still: you!"

Nature

Well, that's her, that's how she is: Nature, and the spirit
refuses to know her.
There's the meadow, hung with the scent of honey
and a whiff of swamps,

And the beginning wail of the wind,
like wolves in the distance,
and up over the fringes of pine
piebald clouds come galloping by.

I see shadows, appearances,
and anger takes me and I see
only the empty likeness, the barren variations
in the Creator's seeds, spilled over the earth.

Oh Earth, stop your games!
Throw off your beggar's rags and
stand, as you really are, a star
filled with fire, and burning!

Creation

My words spawned giants,
and they sat guzzling wine
all night, crimson wine,
horrible wine.

I would not have known such weariness
had they been drinking my blood;
Dawn's fingers were running across
my back when I fell asleep.

I woke when it was evening.
The swamps were breathing mist,
a heavy, uncomfortable breeze
blew warm from the southern gates.

And suddenly I felt an immense wound,
an intense sorrow that there had been a day
without me, a day that passed while I slept,
passed and was gone where it pleased . . .

If I could run where the light went, and catch it!
But I have no power
to rip up this sinister notebook,
my book of dark phantoms and visions of night.

Stockholm

I dreamed of Stockholm: why?
A restless, troubled dream
sprung from some different time,
almost a nightmare—almost . . .

A holiday, maybe: who knows?
The bell kept clanging, that bell,
like a huge organ gone mad,
and a whole city praying, buzzing, roaring . . .

I stood on a hill, ready
to preach. About what? To whom?
I saw the clear water,
trees, forests, fields.

"Oh God!" I cried, frightened. "What if
this is my country, this?
What if I lived here, and loved, and died,
here in this sun-filled green place?"

And I knew that I was forever lost
in the blind corridors of space and time,
and that somewhere Russian rivers were flowing
but I, I would never see them, never.

Sweden

Land of quick cold,
of forests and heavy-backed mountains, where
rumpled waterfalls
roar like prophets of doom—

Sacred land, sacred forever,
do you still remember
when your grim-faced Varangians
went out across Europe to Greece?

Is it right? Can it be right
that Oleg's bronze shield,
having seen so much bloodshed, could be
abandoned at Constantinople's golden gates?

Can your Russian sister, helped
by your hands to glory, to power, to triumph,
wilt her head, again,
in a torment of madness?

Can your fresh northern wind
have howled sweetly but emptily
in our ears? Did your Rurik waste his years
in Russia, build his empire for nothing?

You and Me

Sure, I'm not good enough,
I come from the provinces,
I don't strum a guitar
but blow an old reed flute.

I don't read poems in velvet rooms and red-plush
halls, to dark dresses and starched black coats;
I read to waterfalls, I read to dragons,
I read to clouds.

When I'm in love—it's like a bedouin
falling on his face when he finds water,
not like a knight in a picture
staring up at the stars—and waiting.

I won't die in a bed
with a doctor and a lawyer puffing up my pillow,
but in some narrow ditch,
covered with wild ivy,

And the Heaven I'll go to won't be the hygienic
Protestant paradise, open to everyone,
but that Heaven where whores and robbers and Judean
tax collectors will yell: Hey! Come out of that ditch!

Ice Floes and the River Neva

Transparent spring green
was sprouting on the islands—
but no, the Neva's fickle,
and turns gloomy in a flash.

On the bridge: look.
Ice floes jumping, green
like copper poison,
rustling, as terrible as snakes.

Our dreams sweat, and labor; a geographer's
dreams must press hard on him, now,
the agonized outlines
of unknown continents—

Like hidden vaults
where the corpse is buried and the toads crawl,
cellars smelling of damp mushrooms,
uncertain, faint.

The river's sick, it's mad.
Only the polar bears in our zoo
are happy, sure
they'll win,

Knowing their cages are a painful
fiction, a lie, knowing
the Arctic Ocean is coming
to free them, the ocean itself.

Childhood

I loved the great meadows
and their honey scent
and clumps of trees, and dry grass
and bull's horns in the grass.

Every dusty bush along the road
shouted, "I'm playing with you!
Walk around me, watch out,
and you'll see who I really am!"

Only the fierce autumn wind, roaring,
could stop my games:
my heart would thump, it was heaven itself,
I felt sure I would die

With my friends, never alone,
with soft warm flowers, with cool cold flowers,
and up over those far-off skies
I would guess it all, all at once.

If I love this new game, this war
and its big bangs,
it's simply that human blood is no more sacred
than the emerald juice from a blade of grass.

Autumn

An orange sky,
a wind blusters
in the rowan tree;
I chase a horse
past the greenhouse glass,
past the old park fence,
past the swan pond.
My dog runs too,
shaggy red
and dearer than
my brother,
never to be forgotten
even if she dies.
The hooves hit harder,
dust spurts up:
an Arabian horse
is hard to catch.
I'll have to rest, I guess,
collapse breathless on a
heavy flat rock,
wondering dully
at the orange sky,
listening dully
to the wind's piercing scream.

Primal Memories

Life—all of it—there it is! Dancing, singing,
cities, deserts, oceans—
a quick reflection
of what's forever lost.

Fires burn, trumpets blare,
and chestnut horses run,
and nervous lips repeat,
keep repeating—what?—Happiness. Yes, happiness, I think.

And that's ecstasy, and that's pain,
again, once again, forever again;
an ocean waves its grey-haired mane,
deserts sprout, and cities.

And when will I finally end
this dream, and be myself—
a humble Indian dozing
in the sacred twilight, along some quiet river?

A Workman

A red-glowing forge, a small
old man, standing;
red eyelids blinking
and his face submissive, calm.

The others are asleep,
he's alone, busy
casting the bullet that will cut me
away from the earth.

Done—and his eyes grow gayer.
He goes home. The moon is shining;
his wife, sleepy and warm,
lies waiting in a big bed.

His bullet will whistle
across this Russian river,
will find my heart.
It has come to find me.

I will fall, twisting, I will see
history as history was,
while my blood will rush
like a fountain on the dusty, beaten grass.

And the Lord will reward me, yea
in full, for this swift and bitter
life. And this was done by the small
old man in the faded grey blouse.

The Muzhik

In brambles, deep in huge marshes,
near a tin river,
in shaggy log cabins, dark, dark,
there are strange muzhiks.*

Sometimes one comes out, there where no roads go,
where feather-grass * scatters,
and he listens to Stribog * scream, and
he senses an old story, a true story.

A Pecheneg * came through here, once,
staring straight ahead . . .
It smells of snakes, of must and mist,
down near the emptying rivers.

There he is, carrying his pack,
filling the forest trail
with a long, drawn-out song, a soft song,
but a sly song, oh a wicked song.

This trail is—light and darkness,
a thief whistling in fields,
arguments, bloody quarrels
in inns as frightening as dreams.

He comes—God help us!—
to our proud capital.
He enchants the empress
of endless Russia

With his eyes, his childlike smile,
his sly talk—
and a gold cross glows
on his brave chest.

Why didn't the cross on the church
of Kazan,* and Saint Isaac's * cross,
why didn't they—oh Christ our Lord!—
why didn't they bend, and descend?

Shots and shouts across the shaken
capital, bells, alarms;
the city bares its teeth like a lioness
protecting her cubs.

"Well, go on, you holy ones, burn
my corpse on the dark bridge,
throw my ashes to the wind . . .
Who'll defend an orphan?

"In a wild, poor country
there are lots of strange muzhiks.
You can hear their joyful feet rumbling
along your roads, along your roads . . ."

---

* A *muzhik* (pronounced *moo-ZHEEK*) is a Russian peasant. This poem is about
Rasputin. *Feather-grass, Stribog* (the ancient Slavic pagan god of the winds), and
Pecheneg (a nomadic Turkic people of the central Asian plain, sometimes called
Polovtsy) are allusions to the twelfth-century *Tale of Igor's Men* and are therefore
redolent of ancient Rus, of the disastrous history of old Russia. *Saint Isaac's* and *Kazan
Cathedral* are the two largest and most prominent churches in Saint Petersburg. —Ed.

The Winged Victory of Samothrace

In my night-time fever
I see you, O
Winged Victory of Samothrace,
reaching out your arms.

First night-silence runs
from you, then your blind
inexorable driving flight
brings giddiness, whirling sick.

Your crazy-bright eyes
laugh, and blaze,
and our shadows run behind us,
and can't keep up, can't keep up.

Consolation

From the grave
you hear wonderful bells,
you smell
the whitest lilies.

From the grave
you see God's light
and the glowing flight
of seraphim's wings.

You're dying, yes,
your lovely hands are cold,
you don't believe, you don't know
how Heaven flowers,

But you'll go there
because I've prayed, you'll go
to Heaven, I know
you'll go, I swear it.

From *Pillar of Fire* (1918–1921)

The Lost Tram

A strange street, then crows
croaking, then the sound of a lute
and thunder crawling slow
from a distance—then a tram at my feet

And I leaped, somehow, and the railing
held, and I stood, dazed,
stupidly watching a trail
of fire streaking like sunrays.

Rushing like a storm with dark wings
the tram blundered and was lost
in time's pit . . . "Driver, off!
Stop! This minute—listen!"

No. We'd run round the wall,
ploughed a palm grove, clattered
a Neva bridge, a Nile
bridge, a bridge on the Seine,

And seen for a second a beggar
watching with knowing eyes—
the beggar from Beirut, right,
the same: he died

Last year. Where am I? My heart
pumps languid fear: "Did you miss
the station? They sell tickets there
for the India of the Spirit."

A sign . . . Bloody letters
spelling Grocer: better
than turnips or beets they sell
bleeding heads, severed.

The butcher with a face like an udder
and a red shirt takes my head
too and slops it in a box
of heads, at the bottom.

A side street, house with three windows,
wooden fence, a lawn . . .

"Driver, I need to get down
here, stop, this minute!"

Mashenka: you lived here, and sang,
and wove me a rug, and promised
to marry me. Body and voice
where are you? Not dead, not you?

You moaned in your room when I powdered
my hair to present myself
to the Empress. I never
saw you again.

I see: freedom for us
is light from another world;
men and shadows wait
at the gate of the planets' zoo.

And then a sweet familiar
wind, and over that bridge
an iron glove and two hooves
rush toward me.

Saint Isaac's dome on the sky
like God's true hand:
let them sing for Mashenka
and mourn for me.

How can I breathe? It hurts
to live. My heart tears
itself. Mashenka, I never knew
how much love and sorrow we can bear.

The Word

Then, when God bent His face
over the shining new world, then
they stopped the sun with a word,
a word burned cities to the ground.

When a word floated across the sky
like a rose-colored flame
eagles closed their wings, frightened
stars shrank against the moon.

And we creeping forms had numbers,
like tame, load-bearing oxen—
because a knowing number
says everything, says it all.

That grey-haired prophet, who bent
good and evil to his will,
was afraid to speak
and drew a number in the sand.

But we worry about other things, and forget
that only the word glows and shines,
and the Gospel of John
tells us this word is God.

We've surrounded it with a wall,
with the narrow borders of this world,
and like bees in a deserted hive
the dead words rot and stink.

The Master Artists' Prayer

I remember an ancient artists' prayer:
Keep us, Lord, from students

Who push our wretched genius
toward the blasphemy of new revelations.

Honest and open enemies we can deal with,
but this kind hangs in our footsteps

And smiles, and laughs, as we fight—until
Peter forswears, until Judas betrays.

Heaven alone knows our weakness;
the future will measure our secret fear.

What we create in that future is up to God,
but this time that we've made is ours.

We greet our enemies,
And to flatterers we say: NO!

Noisy fame-talk, and fawning critics,
are useless for shaping sacred forms:

How shameful to dull an artist with opium,
like Hannibal's elephant before a battle!

Memory

Snakes shed their skins
and their souls grow mellow.
We do it differently, we change
souls, not bodies.

Like an Amazon, Memory leads life
like a horse on a rope:
Tell me, Memory, who lived
in this body before I came.

The first one: homely, thin,
loving only the twilight of trees,
and dead leaves, a witch-child
who stopped the rain with a word.

His friends: a chestnut dog
and a tree. Oh Memory, Memory,
don't try to tell the world
that child was me.

And next: this one loved the south wind,
and every noise rang lyres in his head;
life was his girl, his friend, he said,
and the rug he stood on—that was the world.

I hate his guts. He wanted
to be God, to be king;
he hung a poet's shingle
on the door of this my silent house.

Ah, but the one who chose freedom, him
I love, the sailor, the marksman:
the sea sang to him,
the clouds were jealous.

His tent rose tall,
his mules ran strong and hard;
he drank the sweet air like wine,
there where white men never walk.

But Memory, from one year to the next
you're feebler: Who's that, next, the one
who traded freedom
for sacred war, long-awaited war? Is that him?

The one who discovered hunger,
bad dreams, an endless, endless path—
but Saint George touched him twice
and never bullets.

I am the stubborn architect
of this dark temple,
I am jealous of our Father's heavenly
glory, and His earthly glory.

Flames roast my heart, will roast my heart
until the new Jerusalem's
clear, pure walls rise
in Russian fields.

And then, a strange wind will blow
—and Heaven will rain a terrible light,
a sudden-blooming Milky Way,
a dazzling planet-garden.

And I will see a stranger, but
not his hidden face—but I'll know, I'll know,
when I see a lion running behind him
and an eagle up over his head.

I'll shout, I'll scream—but who could help me?
My soul will die.
Snakes shed their skins, we change
souls, not bodies.

The Forest

White trunks
were stark, suddenly, against the haze,

Roots wound up out of the ground
like corpses' arms.

The leaves' bright fire
hid giants, dwarves, lions;

Fishermen saw in the sand
the print of a six-fingered hand.

No French noble, no knight of the Round Table,
ever walked here.

No robber slept in these bushes,
no monk dug caves in these hills.

Once, one stormy night,
a woman with a cat's head came out of this forest,

Wearing a silver crown,
but she moaned all night

And died at dawn
before a priest could save her soul.

Ah, but that was so long ago
that no one remembers,

That—that was in a land
your dreams won't take you to.

And I invented all this, staring
at your braids, the coils of a flaming snake,

Your green eyes
like round Persian turquoise.

That forest—it might be your soul.
That forest—it might be my love—

Or maybe, when we die,
that forest is where we'll go, together.

Bird-Girl

Early one morning
in Broseliana
a happy shepherd
drove his flock to the valley.

They grazed, and he
piped out his happiness
on a reed
pipe.

And suddenly, there in the branches,
he heard a voice, not a bird-call,
and saw a flame-red
bird with a tiny girl's head.

It sang, then stopped, then sang,
then stopped, like a baby crying in its sleep.
Its lazy black eyes reminded him
of Indian slaves.

He stared
hard:
"A beautiful bird
but such bitter moaning."

And then, confused,
he hears it say,
"Nowhere on the green earth,
nowhere, is there another

"Like me. But here in Broseliana
a male bird is supposed
to be born, filled
with mysterious longing,

"And think, shepherd:
fate is vicious, refuses us
happiness, for I
must die for him to be born.

"And why should I sing
the sun, or the high new moon?

Nobody needs my songs,
my lips, my pale white cheeks.

"And him, I'm sorriest
for him, for it's him I love
best, and without me
how lonesome he'll be!

"He'll fly here, there,
he'll sit in these elms,
he'll call to his mate,
and his mate will be dead.

"You're not much, shepherd,
but I don't care, I understand pain:
come, kiss
my lips, my delicate white neck.

"You're young, you'll marry,
you'll father children,
and then the Bird-Girl
will be remembered, will fly down the centuries . . ."

He breathes the scent
of her sun-warmed skin,
he hears gold bracelets
ringing on her claws,

And mad,
wild, almost unconscious,
his rough knees
smash down on her red feathers.

She moaned just once, just
once, before
her heart
stopped.

And dead is dead:
her eyes blur,
the shepherd pipes funeral songs
over her body.

Twilight.
Grey mist.
He drives his flock home,
away from Broseliana.

The Sixth Sense

Fine is the wine that loves us,
and the bread baked for our sake,
and the woman who lies and loves us
when she's finished her tweaking games.

But sunset clouds, rose
in a sky turned cold,
calm like some other earth?
immortal poems?

All inedible, non-potable, un-kissable.
Time comes, time goes,
and we wring our hands
and never decide, never touch the circle.

Like a boy forgetting his games
and watching girls in the river
and knowing nothing but eaten
by desires stranger

Than he knows—like a slippery creature
sensing unformed wings
on its back and howling helpless
in the bushes and brambles—like hundred

Years after hundred years—how long, Lord,
how long? —as nature and art
cut, and we scream, and slowly, slowly,
our sixth-sense organ is surgically born.

Soul and Body

Silence hangs across the city,
every tiny sound strikes flat, hollow, remote—
and you, soul, you still say nothing:
oh God, have mercy on marble souls.

And my soul said to me,
like harps singing in the distance,
"Why did I find existence
in worthless human flesh?

"Why did I leave my home,
try madly for some different glory?
The Earth turns and tumbles like a convict's
iron ball-and-chain.

"Ah, I hate love,
that universal earth-disease
which fogs my vision, over and over fogs my vision
of this alien world, this beautiful, ordered world.

"Whatever still ties me to the glow
of the swinging planets
is only sorrow—my faithful shield,
my cold, contemptuous sorrow."

2

A gold sunset turned copper,
green rust spread on clouds,
and I ordered my body
to reply.

And my body answered
(only a body, but a body with hot blood),
"What is this thing, 'existence'?
Love: that I know.

"I splash in salt waves: I love that.
I listen to hawks screaming: I love that.

And I love to gallop on an unbroken horse,
across meadows fragrant with seeds and smells.

"And I love women . . . When I kiss
her eyes, as they look away, look down,
I love her drunkenly, like thunder coming closer,
like clear spring water on my tongue.

"I've taken things, I want things,
and for these, for sorrow, for joy, for wild thoughts,
I will pay, as a man should,
with my own final destruction."

3

And then God's voice flashed
down from the Great Bear,
demanding, "And who are you to ask?"
My soul came to me, and my body.

I watched them, quietly,
then answered their boldness with gentle words:
"Is a dog wise
because it howls at the moon?

"Who are you to ask me? *me?*
All of earth-time, from
start to burning end, is only a moment
for me.

"Like the great root-tree of the world, Yggdrasil,
seven times seven universes have sprouted
in me, my eyes see earth
and heaven as dust.

"I sleep, and the endless depths
cover my unutterable name—
and you, you're a feeble echo from
the lowest level of my being!"

Canzonet One

A red, feathery
fire cried
loud
in my courtyard, into the blue-black of sleep.

A wild, sweet
wind from the moon
blew, lashed at silence,
insolently whipped its bare cheeks.

And walking out on the mountains
the young dawn came
feeding greedy clouds
with amber barley.

I was born at dawn, now,
I will die at dawn—
which is why
I never dream of anything Good.

And my lips are happy
to kiss just one woman,
the one I don't need
to fly with, off into empyrean heights.

Canzonet Two

We're not in this world—we're somewhere
in the world's backyard, under the trees, where
sleepy summer turns the
blue pages of clear days.

A coarse, busy pendulum,
time's hidden sweetheart,
chops off conspirators' heads
(pretty heads), swish, done!

Roads are so dusty,
bushes want so much to be dry, here,
that seraphim won't
bring us any more unicorns.

My love, only in your lonely secret sorrow
is there any fierce, dulling pleasure—
and in this damned, godforsaken place
it's like a wind from faraway lands.

There, everything moves, there, everything
sparkles, sings—we're there, you and I, we live
there. What's here is our reflection
in a stagnant pond.

Persian Miniature

When I've given up
playing at hide-and-seek with sour-faced
Death, the Creator will turn me
into a Persian miniature—

With a turquoise sky
and a prince just raising
his almond eyes
to the arc of a girl's swing,

And a bloody-speared Shah
rushing down rocky paths,
across cinnabar heights,
after a flying deer,

And roses that no eyes,
no dreams have ever seen,
and vines bending into the grass
in the sweet twilight,

And on the other side,
clean as clouds in Tibet,
a great artist's mark:
a sign and a joy.

Some fragrant old man
of business, of the court,
will see me, love me
at once, love me hard and sharp.

His dull-turning days
will wind around me.
Wine will vanish for him,
and women, and friends.

And finally—without ecstasy,
without pain—my old dream
will be satisfied,
and everyone, everywhere will adore me.

The Drunken Dervish

Nightingales in the cypresses, the moon over the lake:
black stone, white stone, my skin is full of wine.
The bottle sang, it sang louder than my heart:
the world is light from my friend's face, everything else is its shadow.

It wasn't yesterday, it wasn't today, that I learned to love wine;
it wasn't just yesterday, it wasn't just today, that I was drunk by dawn.
And I stagger and strut that I know ecstasy:
the world is light from my friend's face, everything else is its shadow.

I'm a tramp, I live in bushes, I'm a bum,
I've forgotten forever whatever I ever learned,
all for a rose-red wry smile and a song:
the world is light from my friend's face, everything else is its shadow.

Here I am, walking on my friends' graves,
why can't I ask corpses about love?
And a skull shouts secrets out of its hole:
the world is light from my friend's face, everything else is its shadow.

Rivers rock in the smoky lake, under the moon,
nightingales no longer sing in the tall cypresses,
but one sang loudest, just one, the one who did not sing at all:
the world is light from my friend's face, everything else is its shadow.

The Leopard

If a dead leopard's whiskers are not
singed at once, his spirit will haunt
the hunter who killed him.
   —ABYSSINIAN SAYING

The leopard I killed
is busy with witchcraft, with reading
palms, here in my room
in the silence of hollow nights.

People come and people go,
and the last one
is the one for whom golden darkness
runs in my veins.

It's late. Mice are whistling,
the house spirit grunts tonelessly,
and the leopard I killed
purrs next to my bed.

—Dobrobran: long ravines,
dove-colored mist,
and the sun, red like a bullet-hole,
lighting up Dobrobran.

—Wind, driving east the scent
of honey, of verbena,
and hyenas howl, howl,
digging their noses in the sand.

—Brother, brother: do you hear them howling,
do you smell that fragrance, do you see that smoke?
Then why do you breathe
this damp air?

—Murderer: you must
die where I died,
so I can be born again
as a leopard . . .

Do I have to listen
till dawn comes?
I didn't listen, I didn't
singe his whiskers!

Too late! That angry power has beaten me,
it's coming, coming closer:
a hand, there, a copper hand
squeezes my head . . .

Palm trees . . . a terrible fire
burns the sand, pours from the sky . . .
Danakil crouches behind a rock,
waiting with a flaming spear.

He neither knows nor asks
what my soul may be proud of,
he'll throw this soul,
not knowing what or where.

And I can't fight, I'm too weak.
I get up, calm.
I will die
at this well where giraffes drink.

My Readers

An old tramp in Addis Ababa,
conqueror of many tribes,
sent me a black lance-bearer
bringing a greeting of my own poetry.
A lieutenant who runs gunboats
under enemy cannon
read me my poems, for a souvenir, one whole night
across the southern sea.
A man who shot the Tsar's
ambassador, killed him in a crowd,
shook my hand,
thanked me for my poems.

Many of them, many of them—strong, vicious, gay,
killers of elephants, killers of people,
dead in deserts,
frozen at the edge of eternal ice—
as it should be, on this
strong, gay, vicious planet—
and they carry my poems in their saddlebags,
they read them in palm groves,
forget them on sinking ships.

They're not insulted with sick nerves, in my poems,
not embarrassed by my heartfelt feelings,
not bored with pregnant hints
about what's left in an egg when it's eaten:
but when bullets whistle,
when waves crack in ships,
I teach them not to be afraid,
not to be afraid, and to do what must be done.

And when a beautiful woman,
the only woman in their world,
says: Not you, I don't love you,
I teach them to smile
and leave and never come back.
And in their last hour,
when a red mist spreads across their eyes,
I'll teach them how to remember

all their cruel, lovely lives, all
at once, and their country, loved and
strange, and how to stand in God's
presence and speak simple, wise words,
and wait, calm, for His Judgment.

Posthumous and Uncollected Poems

The White Willow (1920)

The white willow was black, up on the hill,
crows puffed faintly;
in the blue, the very blue meadow
clouds wandered like sheep.
And intending to give yourself
you said, "I love you—"
and grass grew all around, grass like an ocean,
and it was afternoon.
I was kissing love letters from summer,
grass-shadows on your sun-warm cheeks,
the fragrant festival of light
in your bronze hair.
And I wanted you, you
were a fantastic new country,
a promised land
of ecstasy, of songs, of wine.

My Hour (1919)

It's not dawn yet,
not night, not morning.
A crow under my window,
half awake, lifts one wing,
and in the sky star after star
melts forever.
Now: this is my hour, I can do anything—
my mind can reach through to a helpless enemy
and leap on his chest
like a nightmare lion—
or come to a girl's bedroom
down corridors only angels know,
and deep in her drowsy memory
cut through oblivion like a beam of light
and burn my face
like a symbol of Beauty.

But the world is quiet, so quiet
that I hear night animals walking
and the owl's wings
wandering forever in the high air.

And somewhere the ocean's dancing,
and there's a white mist above it
like smoke from a sailor's pipe,
a sailor whose corpse is almost buried in the sand.
This pre-dawn breeze
flows, gay, cruel,
insanely gay—like me,
and as cruel as my fate.
Sharing another's life: Why should I bother?
Can I drain my own?
Will even my whole will open
a single stalk, a single stem for me?

You, sleeping all around me,
you who do not meet day as it comes,
in return for my mercy to you,
my burning my hour alone,
leave tomorrow's darkness too
for me, alone.

A Knight of Happiness (1917–1918?)

How easy the world comes!
You—angry at life,
you—sighing like the wind,
I can make everyone happy.

Come: I'll tell you
about a green-eyed girl,
and the blue darkness of morning,
shot through with poems and light.

Come! I'll tell you, I need
to tell, over and over,
how sweet life is, how sweet to win
oceans and women, to conquer enemies and words.

And if you don't understand,
or won't,
and moan about sorrow
and pain—pistols or swords?

A Little Song (1917–1918)

That scent is you,
        only you,
you move, you shine
        like the moon.

Things you've touched
        are holy,
blessed with a new
        beauty.

Who can bother
        worrying,
can keep from wanting
        you?

The pain-pure sky
        of your eyes,
the fairy-tale foam
        of your arms—

The world is women,
        and is men,
but only one man has what he wanted:
        only me.

(1917)

You'll still remember me—still,
and my strange, moving world
of nonsense and songs and fire,
the only honest world in our world.

It was yours, had you wanted. Was it
too much, my world? Too little?
Maybe I wrote bad poems
and prayed—I shouldn't have prayed—for you.

But you'll bend, all boneless, and say,
"No, I don't remember, I can't,
I'm caught in another world
of rough, simple beauty."

My Days (1917)

My days blow dully
by, as painful as ever,
like a rose-petal rain,
like nightingales dying.

But she too knows pain,
she who commanded
my love, and her satin skin
flushes with poisoned blood.

And if I stay alive
it's all for a single
dream: like two blind children
we'll climb a mountain,

Up there where only goats
walk, a world of the whitest
clouds, and we'll hunt for wilted
roses, we'll listen to dead nightingales.

A Portrait (1917)

Only a diamond
left lying on black velvet
shines
like her almost singing eyes.

The unfocussed white
of her porcelain body
torments, like lilac petals
in dying moonlight.

And if her arms are gentle wax, their
blood flows just as hot
as the eternal candle
in front of Mary's icon face.

And she is all so light, like an
autumn bird
ready, oh ready to say goodbye
to a sad northern country.

(1914)

When the pain has drained me,
and I stop loving her,
from somewhere pale hands
come covering my soul.

And someone's sad eyes
call me softly back,
burning with some other earth's entreaty
in the cool night darkness.

And weeping with pain,
cursing at God and myself,
I kiss those pale hands,
those quiet eyes.

You

No one's more restless, no one's more capricious,
but I gave myself to you, oh long ago,
because when you choose to you blend
many, many lives into one.

And today: grey sky,
a weary dull day, and long,
and out in the park, on the wet grass,
there were no children playing leapfrog.

You sat looking at old prints,
head propped on your hand,
and all the idiotic figures
marched dully by.

"Look, my dear: a bird.
And here's a man on a fast horse.
But what a strange frown
on this fat alderman's face!"

And later you read me a prince's story,
a gentle prince, pious, pure,
and as you turned the pages
the tip of your little finger touched my sleeve.

But when the day-noises stopped
and the moon rose over the city,
you suddenly twisted your hands together
and turned miserably pale.

And confused, shy, I
said nothing, but I dreamed this:
that you too could hear the sweet violin
singing of a golden paradise.

Stories

African Hunt

FROM A TRAVEL DIARY

I

Old maps used to show Africa as a girl, rough and yet somehow beautiful—and always, always surrounded by wild animals: monkeys swinging over her head; elephants swishing their trunks behind her back; a lion licking her feet; and beside her, lying on a sun-warmed rock, a lazy panther soaking in the bright light.

The old painters didn't deal with the spread of colonization, or with the building of railroads, or with irrigation, or with drainage earthworks. And they were right: only in Europe do we think that the battle between Man and Nature is over—or that, anyway, the odds are decisively in our favor. It does not seem that way, once you have been in Africa.

Railroad embankments, narrow and precarious, are washed away every summer, when the rain pours down. Elephants like to scratch themselves on the nice smooth telegraph poles—and snap them like toothpicks. Riverboats are regularly overturned by hippopotamuses. The English have been busy conquering the Somalia peninsula for years; they're still not a hundred kilometers in from the shore. And yet, for all this, you can't say that Africa is inhospitable: whites can enter her forests just as easily as blacks, and by silent agreement an animal will hold back and let an approaching man come to a waterfall first. Guests, yes—guests are welcomed, but not as hosts, not as masters.

A European who can get through the chain of whining skeptics (most of them petty traders) in seaside cities—who can keep from listening to the ominous warnings of his country's diplomats—who can manage to put together a caravan of reasonable size, neither bulky nor cumbersome—can still see Africa as she was thousands of years ago, nameless rivers with lead-heavy waves, deserts where only God would dare to raise His voice, rotten forests hidden in high mountain gorges and waiting to fall at the first tiny shock. He can hear the lion, crouching for his spring, hitting his sides with his heavy tail, and he can hear the claw hidden in that tail ring out as it clangs on his ribs. He can marvel at the Shangalians, among whom no woman can walk, in the presence of men, except on all fours. If he is a hunter, he can find game worthy of the princes in fairy tales. But he must also harden himself in both body and in spirit—in body, to hold back fear of desert heat and rotting wet swamps, fear of ever-possible injury, fear even of starvation; in spirit, to keep from trembling at the sight of blood, both his and others', and to learn to accept this new world so unlike the one we live in, and to accept it as it is, enormous, terrible, and marvellously beautiful.

2

The Red Sea, too, is clearly a part of Africa. And hunting sharks in the Red Sea is a fine way to be introduced to African hunting.

We dropped anchor outside Jedda. There was no going in, since there was plague. I know nothing more beautiful than the bright green coral reefs of Jedda, edged with faintly rose-colored foam. Perhaps the *hadji,* the Muslims who have made the holy pilgrimage to Mecca, wear green turbans in their honor?

While they were taking on coal, we decided to hunt sharks. We used a huge hook, tied to a strong cable and loaded with ten pounds of rotten meat, as a fishing rod. A log was the float. But we couldn't see any sharks: either there weren't any, or else they had swum so far off that their pilot fish couldn't spot the bait. Sharks are very nearsighted, so they always travel with two pretty little fish who steer them to food and then take a share for their services.

Finally we saw a dark shadow in the water, perhaps ten feet in length, and the float whirled around a few times, then plunged under-water. We jerked up the cable—but all we got was the hook, the meat still on it. The shark had just tugged at it, he hadn't tried to swallow it. And now, upset and angry because his appetizing meal had dis-appeared, he was charging about in circles, splashing the water with his tail. The pilot fish, confused, were rushing this way and that. We threw the baited hook back in, as quickly as we could. This time the shark rushed at it, not hesitating a moment. The cable pulled taut, looked as though it might snap, then went slack, and out of the water came a round, shining head with small, malicious eyes. I've seen eyes like that before, but only on old and particularly ferocious wild boars. There were ten sailors pulling on the cable, and sweating. The shark was spinning madly about; we could hear his tail smashing against the side of the ship, churning in the water like a propeller. The chief mate leaned over the railing, aimed his revolver, and fired five bullets into him. The shark leaped, then went calm. There were five black holes in his head and his whitish lips. The men heaved, and the terrible carcass came to the side of the ship. Someone touched his head, and he clanked his teeth, snapping—not dead at all, in fact quite fresh and resting, bracing himself for the final battle. The mate tied a knife to a long stick and, with a strong, straight, accomplished blow, drove it into the shark's chest and, straining fiercely, ripped the slit down to the base of the tail. Blood and water came spurting out, and a pink spleen perhaps four feet long, and a large spongy liver, and yards of intestines rolled out and began to rock in the quiet water, like unknown new jellyfish, never seen by man.

It was easier to pull him up, now, he was light and easy and they had him on the deck quickly. Swinging a hatchet, the ship's cook began to chop at his head. Someone yanked out his heart: still pulsating, it leaped now here, now there, hopping like a frog. The air was full of the smell of blood.

And down there in the water, right alongside the ship, the orphaned pilot fish swam around and around. Just one of them: the other had disappeared, probably making for some distant bay, to hide there his disgrace, his involuntary betrayal. But this one, this one was inconsolable, faithful to the end, jumping out of the water, over and over, as if to see what they were doing up there with its master. Other sharks were swimming greedily toward the floating guts, and the pilot fish swam spinning around them, expressing in every way it could its ultimate despair.

To get at the teeth, they chopped off the shark's jaws, then threw all the rest into the sea. The sunset, that night, over the green coral reefs of Jedda, was far-flung, bright yellow with the vermilion of the sun at its center. Later it turned to delicate ash, then went green, as if the sea were now reflected in the sky. We raised anchor and sailed directly towards the Southern Cross.

3

There, where the Abyssinian plateau turns into lowlands, and the burning desert sun warms the flat, round rocks, and the shallow caves, and the low shrubs, you often find a leopard, usually a lazy one, lying asleep in the fields near some village. Graceful, parti-colored, enjoying a thousand tricks and whims, he plays in the life of these villagers the role of some glorious, malevolent house demon. He steals their goats and their pigs, and sometimes their children, too. Every single woman among them, if she gets the chance, will come back from fetching water at the spring and report that she saw him resting, high on the cliff, and that she saw him getting ready to spring. Young warriors sing songs comparing themselves to him, and they try to leap as lightly as he leaps. And from time to time some ambitious man goes out hunting him, carrying only a poisoned spear, and if he isn't crippled for life—and often he is—he brings the satiny hide, traced with its intricate, ingenious pattern, to the neighboring trader, and carries home, triumphant, a bottle of bad cognac. A new leopard comes to settle where the dead one had been, and the whole thing starts again, right from the beginning.

Once, towards evening, I came to a small Somalian village, somewhere on the edge of the Hararian hills. My guide, a quick-legged Hararite, ran at once to the elder of the village, to let him know what an important guest he had, and the elder came out to me as quickly as he could, carrying presents of eggs, and milk, and a nice half-year-old kid. As usual, I began to ask him what there was to hunt. He told me that a leopard had been seen on the slope of a neighboring knoll, and not half an hour earlier. He was an old man, and I could believe him. I drank some milk and set out; my guide pulled the kid along behind him, for bait.

The knoll was covered with faded, burnt-out grass, and small, thorny shrubs; it looked like one of our garbage dumps. We tied the kid in the center of a clearing, I settled down in a bush about fifteen paces away, and behind me my Hararite lay down, with his spear. His eyes were bulging and he waved his weapon about, assuring me that this would be the eighth leopard he had killed; he was a coward, and I told him to shut up.

It didn't take long—I was surprised that the kid's desperate bleating didn't collect all the leopards in the whole province. Suddenly I noticed how a bush in the distance stirred faintly, how a rock fell out of place, and I saw the parti-colored beast coming rapidly closer. He was about the size of a hunting dog, and ran on bent legs, pressing his belly to the ground and waving the tip of his tail faintly from side to side. His blunt cat's muzzle was motionless and threatening. And he looked so terribly familiar, from books and from pictures, that for a moment I had the absurd notion that perhaps he had escaped from some travelling circus. Then all at once my heart began to pound, my body straightened of its own accord, and hardly aiming, I fired.

The leopard jumped three or four feet, then fell heavily on his side. His hind legs were jerking, digging up the earth; his front ones were tucked up, as if preparing to spring. But his body did not move, his head kept bending further and further to one side: the bullet had broken his spine, just behind the neck. I realized that he would not attack, and I lowered my gun and turned back to my Hararite. He was gone, his spear was lying in the grass. And then far behind me, out over the slope, I saw a man in a white shirt running desperately in the direction of the village.

I walked up to the leopard; he was already dead, whitish dregs had clouded his still eyes. I wanted to carry him back with me, but at the touch of his soft, almost boneless body, I flinched. And suddenly fear grew in me, like a viscous fever—the reaction to my powerful nervous upsurge, at sight of him approaching. I looked around in back of me: it was turning powerfully dark, almost all I could see was the fading yellow edge of the sky, yellowed by the rising moon. The shrubs rustled with their thorns, hills and knolls arched on every side of me. The terrified kid had run as far as the taut rope would let him, and he stood there, head down, silent now, numb with terror. I felt that all the animals in Africa were lying in a vast circle, around me in the darkness, lying and waiting for their chance to kill me, agonizingly and horribly, shamefully.

And then suddenly I heard the quick tramp of feet, and brief, abrupt shouts, and like a flock of crows a dozen Somalis flew into the clearing, their spears at the ready. They had been running hard, and their eyes were red with exertion; their necks and foreheads were covered with shining drops of sweat, like glass beads. And running after them, gasping for breath, came my guide, my Hararite. He had roused the whole village with the news of my death.

4

The river Awash, first wide and slow, then narrow and boiling like a mountain stream, is entirely surrounded by forests. Not the kind of gloomy, damp forest that runs on for hundreds of miles, but forest-oases, like the kind folk songs sing of, full ringing streams, bright sun, and clear birdcalls. On broad grassy meadows buffalo graze, and in the swamps there are wild boars, hiding deep in thickets. People come there to hunt, come from the East and the West—and from the North, and from the Danikil Desert, come the lions—all of them hunting, lions and men.

And they do not usually meet, men and lions, because some of them hunt in the daylight, some of them hunt at night. When the sun is out the lions sleep high on the hills and, like guards on a watchtower, they watch for miles around. If a man comes near they run quietly down the other side of the hill, and slip away. And at night the people burn fires in a ring around their camps. Each stays out of the way of the other.

But once, in one of these forests, at high noon, when I was amusing myself hunting marabou storks, my guide—a huge, knowing Abyssinian with a pockmarked face—pointed out a track at the edge of the water.

"*Anbassa*—lion," he declared, lowering his voice. "He comes here to drink."

I was doubtful. A lion might drink here tonight, but who could guarantee that he would come to this same place tomorrow? But my guide picked up a whitish, hard little ball, proving that the lion had been here many times. I was convinced. Killing a lion is the secret dream of any white man who comes to Africa; it does not matter if he is a rubber buyer, or a missionary, or even a poet. We discussed the question, my guide and I, and decided to build a scaffold in a tree, and spend the night there. That way the lion could come closer—and shooting from above is usually more accurate.

We found a good spot, not too far away, on the edge of a small clearing. We worked all afternoon, until it grew dark, putting up a clumsy, slanting scaffold on which the two of us could somehow find enough room to sit, with our feet hanging over. To keep from having to shoot, and perhaps frightening the lion off, we caught a turtle, two feet long, and had its liver, roasted on a small campfire, for supper. When it was full darkness we were in our places, waiting.

We waited a long time. At first what we heard was the sound of wild boars, out later than they should have been, turning in the bushes, and then some restless bird cried out, and then it grew so quiet that the whole world seemed to have become empty, deserted, all at the same time. Later on the moon rose, and we saw a porcupine in the middle of the clearing, sniffing the air carefully, and digging a bit in the ground. But just then a hyena gave a loud, rolling cry and the porcupine ran, with mincing steps, into the bushes. My legs were growing terribly numb. We sat like that for perhaps five hours.

Only someone who has traveled can understand what tiredness really is, and how it feels to want sleep desperately. Twice I almost fell from my tower; at last, sour and worn out, I decided to climb down. Better to let the hunting go until tomorrow, better to get plenty of sleep during the day . . . I lay down on my face, in the bushes, my gun beside me; my guide stayed up in the tree. Exceedingly tired people do not fall asleep right away. First there is a heavy torpor, and

I lay unable to move, hearing distant rustling, feeling how the moon was inclining and turning pale.

Suddenly I woke, as if someone had hit me. Only later did I realize that my guide had been whispering, from up in the tree, *"Geta! Geta!"* ("Master! Master!") At the far end of the clearing I saw a lion, black against the background of dark bushes. He was coming out of a thicket, and all I could see was a huge head, held high above a chest broad as a shield. The next moment I fired. My Mauser bellowed incredibly loud, in that utter silence, and like an echo I heard the crash of breaking bushes and the quick leaping noise of an animal running away. My guide had already jumped down from the tree and was standing beside me, his Berdan rifle raised and ready.

Fatigue vanished as if it had never existed. Hunter's madness gripped us both. Running by way of the bushes, we circled the clearing—not daring, still, to go straight—and began to inspect the place where I had seen the lion. We knew that a lion runs away, when shot at, only if he is either seriously wounded or else not wounded at all. Lighting match after match, we crawled around on all fours, looking for drops of blood in the grass. There weren't any. The forest wonder had gotten away with his chestnut hide, his voice of thunder, and the immensely imposing bliss of his steel and velvet movement.

At dawn, we ate the rest of the turtle for breakfast.

5

My young and wealthy Abyssinian friend, Lord Adenu, invited me to visit his estate.

"Oh, it's only two days from Addis Ababa," he assured me. "Only two days, and by a good road."

I accepted, and ordered my mule saddled for the morning. But Lord Adenu insisted that we ride horses, and led up five from his own herd for me to choose from.

I understood why, two days later, when we had covered at least a hundred and fifty miles. In two days!

I was tired, and my tiredness made me miserable, so Lord Adenu proposed that we have a hunt, and not just a simple hunt, but a *battue,* with beaters in the brush, driving out the game.

A *battue,* deep in a tropical forest—it is a completely new experience, utterly unlike anything else. You stand there, waiting, not knowing what will come out from behind this round bush, what will run flashing between this crooked mimosa and that thick plane tree; not knowing which of those with hooves or claws or fangs will run out at you, head lowered, ready for you to link it to your consciousness with a bullet. Who knows, maybe fairy tales don't lie, maybe there really are dragons . . .

We stood along both sides of a narrow ravine, ending in a blind alley. The beaters, about thirty quick-footed Galla people, went deep into that blind dead end. We aimed our rifles at the rocks, there in the middle of the almost vertical slopes, and listened to the voices, moving away from us, now up above, now below, and suddenly all the voices merged into a single triumphant howl. They had found an animal.

It was a great striped hyena, running along the opposite slope only a few yards above Lord Adenu's head. Behind it, swinging a club, rushed the head beater, a thin, muscular, completely naked Negro. The hyena would turn and snap at him, and he would fall back several steps. Lord Adenu and I fired at the same time. Gasping for breath, the Negro stopped, deciding that he had done his part of the job. Turning a somersault, the hyena flew down within two or three feet of Lord Adenu, snapping at him, in the air, as it fell, then somehow managed to get to its feet and start to trot briskly away. Two more shots finished it off.

In a few minutes there was another shout, another animal had been found, but this time the beaters had to deal with a leopard, and they did not run up so daringly or come so close.

With a few mighty leaps the leopard climbed to the top of the ravine, and from there he could run where he pleased. We never saw him, Lord Adenu and I.

Then, for the third time, we heard the beaters shout, but not nearly so clear, this time, and with laughter mixed in. A herd of baboons came up from the bottom of the ravine, and we did not shoot. It was too funny, watching these half-dogs, half-people, running with that clownish clumsiness that only monkeys move with, in flight, only monkeys of all animals. In back of the herd a few old males came running, grey haired, lion maned, their yellow fangs bared at us. These were animals in the full sense of the word, not like the others, and I fired. One of them stopped, began to bark hoarsely, then slowly closed his eyes and sank down on his side, like a human being getting ready for sleep. The bullet had touched his heart; when we walked up to him he was already dead.

The *battue* ended. Lying on a straw pallet, that night, I lay awake for a long time, wondering why I felt no pangs of conscience, killing animals for my own amusement; wondering why my blood tie with the world became stronger, not weaker, because of these killings. And when I slept I dreamed that, because I had taken part in some Abyssinian palace coup, and the coup had failed, they had chopped off my head—and I, bleeding profusely, had applauded the executioner's skill, rejoicing that it was all so simple, so good, and not at all painful.

[*first published August 1916, date of composition unknown*]

The Black General

FOR NATALIA SERGEYEVNA GONCHAROVA

In fact, his father had sold cloth and carpets. But no one dared to remember that, when he came home from Cambridge, because the Viceroy himself received him.

At London soirées, in his student days there, he wore such bright, outlandish clothes, declaimed snatches of the *Mahabharata* so melodiously, declared so sincerely his hatred of everything European, that his success in British society was assured. More than one distinguished old Liberal dowager gave him letters of recommendation (and he took them) when he returned to Bombay (on a second-class ticket).

The rajah of his native state, shaken by his splendid leather suitcases, offered him his choice of posts, either tax collector for in-transit caravans, or the military rank of General. It was generally expected that he would choose to be tax collector, because there were many caravans, and there were not many soldiers. He chose to be a General. No one knew that the elderly American to whom he had explained the mysteries of yoga had died and left him, in his will, quite as much as he had left his valet—that is, rather a lot.

On the day of his appointment, the General appeared at the rajah's palace. Sly rascal that he was, he had anticipated everything: inside his splendid leather suitcases there was, it turned out, a magnificent General's uniform, completely ready. The whole city gathered to stare at him. His old mother sobbed with pride when he raced by on a specially imported, tinselly motorcycle. And the city's leading portrait painter bribed the rajah's servants with a whole rupee, just for the right to watch through the keyhole. He stared through, long, and patiently, and skilfully, soaking in—as a sponge sucks up water—the details of the General's sumptuous costume and of his incredibly self-worshipping face. And finally he walked off, swaying like a camel—which meant, for him, a reverie of deep creative thought.

The little wooden cups, chiselled like lotus petals, burned with the most delicate, the most vivid pigments; his thinnest brushes flew among the little wooden cups with the speed and grace of a girl's fingers, flying over the keys of a piano. And now a lacquered red wall began to appear, and a heavily blue sky, and in the foreground an inordinately conceited General began to take shape. How white his trousers, how rich the gold embroidery on his full-dress coat, how majestic the feathers on his three-cornered hat! In fact, one got to see such a General, as one saw the lotus in the act of blooming, only once in a hundred years.

A crowd began to assemble, moved, stirred, behind the artist's back. The buzz of their rapture grew louder; they made, and then they relished, the wildest speculations. Most likely, the General would take one look at his portrait and make the artist his Major Domo. Yes, he would allow him to eat in his kitchen the rest of his long life—he would give him a sack with a hundred rupees. And a poet who happened by, a tall, bony old man from Tibet, knew the pangs of jealousy and thereupon composed a song, adhering strictly to the rigid rules of Tibetan versification:

The rajah,
The rajah's General,
The rajah's General's full-dress coat,
The girl who will unbutton the rajah's General's full-dress coat,
The love that will immediately possess the girl who will unbutton the rajah's General's full-dress coat,
The son who will be born of the love that took possession of the girl who unbuttoned the rajah's General's full-dress coat.
The throne which will be conquered by the son born of the love that took possession of the girl who unbuttoned the rajah's General's full-dress coat,
The glory that will surround the throne conquered by the son born of the love that took possession of the girl who unbuttoned the rajah's General's full-dress coat,
India, which will be saved by the glory surrounding the throne conquered by the son born of the love that took possession of the girl who unbuttoned the rajah's General full-dress coat:

The song was immediately copied by three scribes, onto a huge sheet of parchment. The General was supposed to pay them.

And here, along the city's quiet streets, terrifying monkeys and peacocks, came the roaring, foul-smelling, tinselly little motorcycle—and the General.

"A Bath!"

And the trained servant from Bombay, who had worked for Europeans before, bowed and waved to a large rubber washbasin, filled with warmish water (because the General was not an athlete and was afraid of cold water). The full-dress coat fell smoothly onto the back of an armchair—unbuttoned, this time, not by a girl, but by the General himself. And next, imitating the full-dress coat, came the white pants with the gold stripe. Only the three cornered hat was belatedly in its proper place when the artists suddenly walked in, the portrait painter in front, the poet behind him, and each carrying his creation aloft. And behind them crowded in a host of admirers, and curious passersby—and among the latter the scribes, who after all had a professional interest in the matter. The General gasped, barked, swore,

"AKH!!!"

and began to shake. Just so, he remembered, a Russian General had gasped, barked, and begun to shake when they had served him unchilled champagne in a restaurant.

"These black . . . What cheek!"

The portrait painter dropped his picture. The General began to jump up and down on it. The Tibetan poem, parchment and all, was torn into shreds. The crowd went numb. The General raved. He leaped about the room like a mad, ferocious monkey; naked, wearing only his three-cornered hat, he yelped and squealed like a jackal with a broken paw. Oh, this was a terrible General.

The servant from Bombay leaned his shoulder against the unwanted guests. Just so, he remembered, European servants pushed away visitors their masters found disagreeable. It only took a minute. The servant was wiping up the floor, because the bath had been overturned, and the General was calming himself down by unpacking his splendid leather suitcases. Ah: with ceremonial slowness he proceeded to hang on the wall an enlarged photograph of himself in his magnificent General's uniform. How sly, he had planned it all, he had had his picture taken before he left London. And under the portrait, smiling happily, he pinned a newspaper clipping, in which his name was mentioned as one of those invited to some social evening. And by this time the servant was hiding the portrait painter's picture, to sell for a farthing to the old-clothes man from Calcutta.

Far away, the scribes, all three of them, all unpaid, were beating the Tibetan poet. And the painter, who had bribed the rajah's servants, expecting to achieve glory thereby, had demanded his money back, and instead they were beating him.

AN EASTERN STORY has to end with a moral. I'll try to disgrace the wicked General. Here he is, arriving in Paris. He has visited the bedrooms of two café *chanteuses,* been received by three socialist members of Parliament, and decided to make a study of the artistic life of France. He stood silent while Anatole France dropped a few caustic remarks. He bought one of Matisse's drawings. He was punched in the face, in some café, by Apollinaire. He even got permission to visit Goncharova's studio, to see her work. And there, there, he saw the Indian portrait painter's picture of him, which had come into her hands via Calcutta, London, and a black Hussar.

Ah, if he had been embarrassed, if he had experienced a delayed repentance! Then my story would be genuinely Eastern. But no, the scoundrel only exclaimed:

"Madame, can you really be interested in such trash? If you like, I can send you a thousand of them, from India."

But he was lying, he'll never send them. Because, thanks to people like him, there are no more artists in India.

Paris, July 1917

The Last Court Poet

Our king was lazy—lazy and just as indifferent as his forefathers had been—and he couldn't bring himself to sign the proper forms, so the old court poet who wrote odes for solemn court occasions could be retired, and have a decent pension. And the poet was stubborn, and would not retire himself.

When there was a birth or a death in the royal family, when a new ambassador arrived from a foreign land, when a new alliance was arranged with another neighboring state, there would first be the usual ceremonies and then the entire court would gather in the throne room and the sullen poet—forever annoyed about something—would begin to read. His archaic language, decrepit words and old-fashioned phrases, was sonorously strange; his old-style powdered wig was pitiful, in that crowd of heads adorned with irreproachable English haircuts and majestically shining bald skulls. The applause that they gave the poet, when his reading was done, was also prescribed by ancient court etiquette; they clapped only with the ends of their gloved fingers, but the noise produced was considered sufficient for the encouragement of poetry.

The poet would make a deep bow, but his face remained gloomy and his eyes sad, even when the king's own hands would reward him with the usual ring, set with a precious stone, or with a gold snuffbox.

And then, when they sat down to the festive dinner, he would take off his powdered wig and sit there, among the old and honorable, the noble and the royal, and talk just as they talked, about railroad concessions, or about the latest theft in the Minister of Foreign Affairs' scandalous office, or he would be vitally interested in some project for a salt tax.

And afterwards, as court etiquette also provided, he would exchange his royal present at the Treasury, and receive a large sum of money, and go back to the large, uncomfortable old house which he had inherited from his father, who had also been court poet. (The late king had made the post hereditary, so that—once and for all—no upstart would ever come to hold it.)

Like its owner's soul, the house was gloomy, dark. The only room that was lit, at night, was his study—lined not with bookcases, but with glass showcases filled with rare antique snuffboxes. The old poet was a passionate collector.

He had been married, once long long ago, and silk dresses had rustled in this dark old house, and slender hands had lovingly turned the pages of beautifully bound books, and the fine old French tapestries, hanging along the walls, had stared at the rose-pink skin, above the gentle décolletage of her dressing gown. But the court poet's wife could not last out even a single year, not in this house: she ran away with some young, unknown artist. And the court poet began a poem in gloomy Byronic stanzas, which was supposed to be about all the joys of revenge—but just then the king's first cousin, once removed, happened to die, and an elegy for this sad occasion had to be written, and after it was written the gloomy Byronic stanzas held no interest, and were abandoned.

Severe, dull, the years dragged on—like gentlemen-in-waiting, squeezed painfully into their full-dress coats—and all that ever happened was the accumulation of more and more new snuffboxes.

Everyone knows that the longer the calm, the worse the storm. But just the same, had the court poet been told how his service to the king was to end, had he been given foreknowledge, his frown would have turned even gloomier and he would have scoffed indignantly, contemptuously, as one does at an inappropriate joke.

It really began, of course, at the banquet in honor of the Spanish prince, newly arrived. One of the guests was an old old nobleman from the old king's time, decrepit, grey haired, toothless and as it happened seated near the court poet. For some reason he had found himself deeply interested in the poet's recitation, just before they all sat down to dinner. He couldn't have heard the verses, of course, since he was stone deaf, but he talked for a long time about how the next-to-last line should have been changed, and suddenly, breaking into a titter, he mouthed a *bon mot* he had probably heard from his great-grandson, to the effect that it had been decided, he had heard, to replace poets with gramophones.

The poet was not really listening. Sitting dreamily, distractedly, next to the old fellow, planning how to enter the conversation on the other side of him, a conversation all about some new Masonic order and how it would operate, he would most likely have thought nothing of the insolent little joke, and forgiven it—but then he saw that the king was looking in their direction and laughing. He said something sharp and crushing to the old man, and as soon as the dinner was over he rose and returned home, even more sullen than usual. And by the next morning he had made up his mind. His servant ran about the whole day, from one book store to the next, buying him books by all the other poets, the "city" poets, as he had always called them, smiling wryly, contemptuously. And for two months, the snuffboxes forgotten, a tense and very secret labor took place, there in the court poet's study. He was learning from his younger brothers, he was sitting at his desk and re-upholstering his style.

But at court everything was peaceful; no one suspected what was being prepared for them in the dark house at the edge of town. The courtiers fell in love, and quarrelled, and grovelled, and did noble deeds, and believed as they had always believed that poetry—well, poetry—I mean, poetry, well, that was just a fossil, left over from the old days, it was just too silly, too solemn for words. And then the day came. A princess of the blood was to be married, roses and ices and verses were sent for. And the court poet was ready. He came right on time, as always, and just as gloomy and unpleasant as ever—and only a really keen observer could have noticed something different, something new about the light, wryly malicious smile quivering faintly at the corners of his mouth, or about the particular, rather unusual nervousness with which he clutched at his verses. But what did anyone care about him, or how he felt, how he had changed? He was too old for the young courtiers; the older and more exalted noblemen, courteous and gracious though they surely were, could not seriously take him as their equal.

The wedding ceremony began. A stately priest went through the ritual quickly, elegantly; the ambassadors came to kiss the new bride's hand; and the court poet, pale, but very determined, began to read. A vague whisper ran through the court. Even the youngest maids of honor, always busily in love with someone or other, raised their pretty heads, astonished, and listened.

What? What? Where are the invocations to the wind-god, the prayer to the eagle, to the wonder-struck earth—all the blossoms of stale old eloquence, where are they? This poetry he was reading, it was new, completely modern, it might even be beautiful—but etiquette had no place for it. This was like the poetry of the "city" poets, whom the court detested, but it was far more brilliant, infinitely more fascinating. It was as if the court poet's talent, so long held in check, so long and so stub-bornly renounced, had suddenly created everything of which it was capable. The lines ran out, breathlessly, running over one another. The rhymes met with the sound of bronze on bronze. Beautiful images soared up like forgotten ghosts from the depths of unknown abysses. The old poet's eyes gleamed like the eyes of an eagle floating high in the sky, and his voice, too, was like an eagle's cry.

What a scandal! In the presence of the entire court, in the very presence of the king himself, to dare to read good poetry. No one had the courage to applaud. The gentlemen-in-waiting, their faces stern, whispered to one another; the young gentlemen of the Royal Bed-chamber lolled back, in an attempt to look unusually sedate, very unusually composed and sedate; and all the shocked ladies raised their thin-pencilled eyebrows with indignant surprise. And the king himself, with a gesture of displeasure, put down the ring he had already taken into his hand, to bestow on the poet.

Quite solitary—as if infected with the plague—the court poet walked out, when his verses were read, and did not bother to wait for the end of the celebration. He could hear the great chancellor ordering the secretary to prepare a decree, at once, for that court poet to be retired, for good.

Ah, but how sweet it was to walk home and to be there alone, truly, completely alone. He walked down the rows of dark halls, proud, sometimes reciting his new poem in a loud voice, sometimes, with a sly, senile, ironical laugh, glancing at the city poets' books. He knew that he had not only matched them, he had even beaten them. And finally, needing to share his happiness with someone, he wrote a letter to his wife—the first since she had left him. Totally triumphant, he reported to her that, at long last, they had not applauded him. He told her that he had now been retired, attached a copy of the poem he'd read, and ended the letter by declaring, with fully understandable pride, "Do you see? *That* is the kind of person you walked out on!"

Princess Zara

A NOVELLA

"Are you really a Zogar, from Lake Chad?" the old woman asked, as he stepped into a patch of moonlight.

He silently uncovered his face and his chest, and the old woman could see powerful muscles under the bronze skin of an African Arab. And she could see, too, the sacred sign on his forehead, given only to especially important messengers. Her old-womanish doubts were put to rest.

"Well, all right," she muttered. "You can trust a Zogar, I know that. You people aren't like these Zanzibar fellows. I wouldn't take one of *them* to the Princess Zara's rooms, you can be sure of that. What's a governor's daughter to them? More of the same kind of merchandise that they load onto their boats, for sale in Constantinople. But that amulet you showed me—it made my old heart beat. After all, I'm from Lake Chad myself. And your gold rings louder, too—it isn't filed down and thin, like ours, after the Jerusalem money lenders are done with it."

The man said nothing. He was pale and apparently tensely absorbed. They crept along the wall, carefully, over the white-cobbled courtyard of the Zanzibar palace.

Near them, very near, but not in sight, the ocean bubbled tonelessly, and the still, heavy tropical night air was damp with the sea's fresh breath. Long silver moon-stripes ran across the water, black in round swimming-places, and reflected in drops scattered, helter-skelter, over the rose-pink marble of the steps. The stars bent down close, very close, confident and lying, like a girl's eyes when she's sinned and wants to hide it. Why has a man from broad meadows and green, thick forests, a strong handsome warrior with a necklace of lion's teeth, why has he come to this world of luxury and sin?

The pages in the book of fates have been jumbled, oh for a long time, and no man can know the strange ways by which death will come to him.

A black archway began to become visible in front of them, as they crawled along the wall, and then a small door, the entrance to the un-married women's half of the harem. A little bronze hammer gave two pre-arranged taps; they could see a young Negro girl's glittering pupils; and then they went in. The lamp's reddish flame was dim, but they could still make out the fairy-tale richness of Persian rugs, covering the floor and the walls, of sandalwood chairs inlaid with ivory, of musical instruments left here and there, carelessly, of phrases from the holy Koran, painted on golden screens in bright green enamel.

She was motionless, light, a fragrance of musk, of Indian perfume, of young flesh. Wrapped in silk, covered in silk, Princess Zara sat on a low, broad ottoman. She seemed made for something nobler, something higher than love: her lips, motionless, seemed carved out of coral, her waist was almost too slender, and her beautiful eyes had a mysterious, sad look. Her arms were bare to the elbow, and she wore gold bracelets around them; a thin band held up her heavy dark hair. And he knew, the stately stranger, that he'd made no mistake in coming.

Bending over, his voice breaking with emotion, he asked the princess to send away her women. Only to her, and to her alone, could he reveal his great secret, carried with him, across smoky lakes and dangerous valleys, here to Zanzibar. Zara said nothing, but the old woman began bustling about, and leading the Negro girl away.

"Don't be afraid," she whispered to the princess. "He won't hurt you. You can trust a Zogar."

And she disappeared, making reassuring winks at the princess, giving a series of little giggles. The Negro girl followed her, like an obedient dog.

He was alone with Zara.

"Who are you?" she asked quietly, so quietly that one could only guess at the beauty, the soft timbre of her voice. "Who are you, why are you here?"

The tall stranger answered, shuddering, "I'm a Zogar, from great Lake Chad, sacred Lake Chad. I'm a chief's youngest son, I am strong among the strong, brave among the brave. Fighting at night, I have killed roaring, gold-maned lions—more than once—and fierce panthers, hearing my step, would run and hide in wild ravines, deep in the bushes, afraid. Many dark-skinned women, women of other tribes, have sobbed over corpses killed by my hands.

"But this once, it was not war drums rolling across the plains. The Zogar people gathered on a knoll, and the great priest drew the sacred messenger's sign on my forehead, and told me how to come to you. I followed the Shari downstream, into the country of the Niam-Niam, ugly little dwarfs who eat each other and pray to a god who lives in a black rock. The poison mists of Ukereva filled me with the flames of jungle fever. Near Ngezi I fought with a huge snake; the Niazi people chased me for forty days. Finally, to my left, I could see the sun sparkling on the snows of Kilimanjaro. The half-moon became a full moon, eight times over, before I reached Zanzibar."

He paused for breath and Zara said nothing, except that with a simple, weary look she asked, "Why?"

And he went on: "The Zogar know the one God, and Allah His Prophet. We are faithful to him, and he is gracious to us. He has given us a very great happiness. The Shining Woman lives in our forests— Allah's favorite and the joy and glory of men. She is divine and she is one and immortal, she can never die, but sometimes she leaves the human shell she has been occupying and reappears in another shell, somewhere in some poor village. And the great priest tells us where she can be found. And whoever is most glorious of all the Zogar is sent to her, and tells her what a shining thing she has become, and then leads her away to the kingdom of emerald green meadows and crimson sunsets. And there she lives, in blissful solitude. Only by great good luck does anyone ever see her. But we pray to her, we do not need to see her: she is our guarantee of the immense nobleness waiting, in the gardens of Allah, for the righteous. If men are strong, and devout, if women are beautiful and true, then only chaste women can have broad, snow-white wings—even though, with our earthbound eyes, we cannot see them. A chaste woman speaks with a voice like an ancient poet's lute, her eyes are as transparent as the water in that sacred spring from which the Prophet drank, when he was in exile. Such women are taller than the virgins granted to men in Paradise, they are taller even than the angels, they are like souls in the seventh circle of the joys of Heaven."

And again he was silent, and Zara did not speak, but her eyes turned mysterious and impenetrable, like the stars that shone down on him, on his journey. His great idea had entirely caught him, he saw nothing, and went on, "You, who call yourself Princess Zara: it is you; the great priest has revealed to us that it is you. You are the Shining Woman of our forests, and I call you to your kingdom. A swift-footed camel, born of a kingly breed, and with hair as silky and white as milk, is waiting for us, impatient, tied to a palm tree. We will run through forests and across plains, like birds flying, we will cross foam-filled rivers, in fast dugout canoes—until, there in front of us, we will see the sacred blue waters of Lake Chad. And on that shore there is a small river valley to which no man can come. And in that valley there are groves of slender palm trees with great broad leaves, hung with ripe orange-colored fruit, trees all crowded around silver-flowing streams, and scented with the fragrance of iris blossoms, and the intoxicating aloe. The sun is caressing and sweet and gentle, there, it does not breathe down with burning heat, its glow blends into the cool freshness of the wind. There, dark gold bees fly down to roses redder than the robes of the ancient kings. There, everything speaks of you, dreams

of you—the sun, and the roses, and the wind. You will live in a beautiful marble cave, and waterfalls as fast as swift horses will delight your
eyes, and golden sand will cover your beautiful feet with kisses, and
you will smile, quietly, at great fantastic seashells. And at sunset, when
a herd of giraffes comes to the watering place, you will stroke the silk
of their regal hides, and they will come to where you stand, to receive
your caresses, to stare into your delighted eyes.

"And there you will live until the moments of happiness begin to
bore you, and you long, like the evening sun, to leave in search of new
incarnations. And then the mighty tribe will gather, as it has gathered
before, to the beating of drums, and again the great priest will reveal
to whoever is most worthy the secret of your new location, your new
disguise. This has happened more than once before, it will happen
more than once, as thousand years follow thousand years.

"But we must hurry. The opalescent moon is falling, falling, it has
dropped to the forest of magnolias, and soon the young sun will rise
out of the rose-colored ocean. Hurry, while the great governor's servants are still asleep. The clear ring of gold will seal the old woman's
lips—and, if not, the Zogar know what a dagger is for."

He was finished. Hopefully, he held out his hands to Zara. Everything was sleepy and quiet in the harem. The only sounds were the
ocean's murmur, somewhere on the other side of the wall, and the sad
cry of some unknown, nervous bird. Slow and flexible like a lily, Princess Zara rose, and stood staring mysteriously at the Arab. And then,
quiet and strange, her words began to rustle, "You spoke well, stranger,
though I don't know what you were talking about. But if you find me
desirable, and you want to love me, I will do whatever you like. You're
much handsomer than that European who, not too long ago, also
bribed his way into the harem. But he said nothing, he just smiled and
made love to me as he pleased. I stood in front of him like a slave he
had bought, but the bitterness of his caresses was sweet, and I wept
when he rode away. And now you are here. If you want me, I am
yours."

She half opened the silk across her breast, she half closed her eyes,
and she waited.

He stared at her, half mad with torment. This was her, the Shining
Woman of the Forests. He had prayed to her all his life, his fathers and
his grandfathers had prayed to her! And there she was, humiliated and
unaware of her disgrace, a sinful smile on her tender lips! Red lightning flashed back and forth across his brain, some triumphant monster
stepped hard on his heart, stepped hard with a hideous, deformed mon-

ster's foot. Wide meadows, long days of gay hunting, all the joy of glory—what was any of it, in the face of this inhuman pain gripping his soul?! His hand happened to touch his dagger. One swift, sure blow into his own chest. Staggering, the powerful soldier's body fell on its face, quivering, twitching, staining the costly Persian carpets with hot blood.

Motionless, still unable to understand what had happened, the compliant princess stayed standing, leaning against the patterned wall. She was proud of her beauty; she had only wanted to find out if her loveliness would stay undefended, humiliated. She had not understood what he was calling her to. And regret was already stirring in her soul, regret for having yielded, as women will, to a dangerous whim, for having lied to him, for having deceived this stranger who had been calling her to some possibly real, dazzling happiness.

And just at dawn a ferocious hyena leaped on the snow-white camel, standing tied to the palm tree, and tore it to shreds.

The Golden Knight

A NOVELLA

In the brilliant gold noon seven crusader knights rode down into a narrow, remote valley in eastern Lebanon. The sun was throwing its multicolored, terrible rays like infidel arrows, the horses were tired from the long journey, and the mighty riders were barely able to stay in their saddles, ready to faint from the intense heat and the intensity of their thirst. And then Oliver, the famous Earl of Canterbury, the oldest among them, gave the sign to rest. And like fragile girls, stunned by the furious, uncontrolled, oppressive violence of the Indian wind, one by one the knights fell helpless on the bare rocks. They were silent for a long time, knowing that they would never rise again, would never mount their horses; knowing that thirst, like a fiery dragon that had climbed up on their chests with its ferocious paws, would soon tear their parched throats apart.

And at last Sir Hugo Elvistam, a Knight Templar with the soul of a Syrian lion, raised himself on his elbow, and called out, "Noble knights, dear brothers in Christ, it is eight days since we lost sight of our friends, eight days since we have wandered alone. And it is two days since we gave our last water to the leprous beggar at the dried-up Well of the Dead Hyenas. But if we must die, let us die like knights, erect, standing on our own feet—and let us sing, this last time, the welcoming hymn to our Heavenly Ruler, Lord Jesus Christ."

And slowly he lifted himself, clutching at thorny shrubs, his eyes unseeing. And one by one his comrades slowly rose, staggering, framing the words with difficulty, like men who had gotten drunk on cypress wine, in cold, dark halls, at some feast given by the Byzantine emperor.

A lone pilgrim, or a merchant from far-off Armenia, would have been startled, and frightened, had they happened to pass by and see seven knights dying in lonely obscurity, had they heard the quiet, harmonious singing.

But suddenly the prayer was interrupted by the light, resonant sound of a horse's hooves approaching, hooves that rung in the desert air like the silver sword in the Archangel Michael's sheath. The knights' proud eyebrows knitted up, and their souls, already friendly with the soft shadows of death, clouded at this unnecessary obstacle. And then, at the turn in the canyon, they saw an unknown knight, slender and strong, beautifully powerful across the shoulders; his helmet visor was down, his armor was of pure gold, as bright as that glittering star, Aldebaran. And his gold horse reared up on its hind legs and jumped, its hooves barely touching the echoing rocks.

A herald, dressed in blue, and mounted on a snow-white horse, hurried after his master. His face was gentle, wise, secretly like the icon face of the apostle John. And these marvellous riders came quickly toward the dying knights, who stood singing their final hymn and waiting.

And the golden knight pulled up his horse and tilted his lance, as though preparing for battle, and the herald raised a shield with a strange coat of arms—mixed lilies and stars, rampant on the pillars of Solomon's temple and prickly blackthorns—and called out the time-honored words for the start of a tournament, "Which of the noble knights, here present this day, will fight with my master, on foot or on horse, with lance or with sword?" And then he rode to one side, and waited.

And suddenly a cooling, quickening wind blew from somewhere, and the slack muscles of the dying knights grew strong again, and the fiery thirst-dragon, who had been tearing at their throats and their chests, turned into a tiny lizard and dropped away, crawling, with an uneasy whistle, into a dark slit in the cliffs, where his brothers, the scorpions and the hairy tarantulas, were hiding.

And Oliver, the Earl of Canterbury, was the first to answer the blue herald, in the name of all his company. In courtly, polite words of great dignity he explained that they could not doubt the unknown knight's noble birth, but that, according to ancient, knightly custom they would like to see him with his visor lifted. He had barely finished speaking when the heavy, gleaming visor was raised and they saw a face of the most perfect beauty that had ever blossomed, on earth or in Heaven, eyes full of bright, pure love, delicate and somewhat pale cheeks, red lips about which Saint Magdalene used so often to dream, and a small golden beard, combed, perfumed by the Virgin Mary herself.

The pious knights were afraid to guess who it was, come to lighten their suffering, to share their sport—but a wave of mystic rapture seized their souls, as a hurricane at sea first seizes frightened swimmers, then whirls them in emerald spray and boiling foam, and finally casts them on the sloping shores of islands of supernatural happiness. Full of awe and reverence and mysterious love for their challenger, they asked him simply to accept the tribute of their respect, before the tournament began.

The first of the knights to come forward was the Earl of Northumber-land—but neither his hands, which had thrown the strongest men to the ground, nor his eyes, which had conquered the most beautiful ladies of merry King Richard's court, could help him. He was jolted out of his saddle, and went submissively off to the side, amazed that his heart, in spite of defeat, was singing and laughing. And one by one his comrades met the same fate. And when the golden stranger, laughing his contagiously merry, gentle laughter, had felled the last of the knights—the Baron of Norwich, huge and mighty, like a bear out of the Pyrenees—with one voice they declared that their opponent's lance had no equal in the entire English army—and, accordingly, no equal in the whole world.

After a tournament there was supposed to be a feast. That was the custom, the time-honored custom, in merry old England. And swept up as they were by the strange knight's charm, they were not at all surprised when, instead of their lances, stuck into the cracks in the cliff, blossoming palms rose up, heavy with seductively ripe fruit, or when a transparent little stream began to run out of the bare rock, ringing like the bronze bracelets of an Arab sheik's favorite daughter.

The weary knights feasted and laughed, talked of battles and of love, and sang harmonious minstrel songs about battles and about love.

And it was sweet, after they had glanced into death's face, to see the sun and the green earth. Every drop they swallowed splashed joy into their wide-open hearts, every bite of food—like bits of a holy sacrament—brought them new life.

Their golden conqueror sat with the others, and he ate and he drank and he laughed.

And in the evening, when the far-away cedars began to whisper among themselves and the shadows brushed down, more and more, against the knights' faces, brushing with their soft wings, the golden knight mounted his horse and rode deep into the ravine. And the others, like men bewitched, followed right after him. And he took them to a wide sloping staircase, made of white marble with tiny blue veins, a staircase ascending straight into the sky. And the sound of earthly horses was heavy on the marble, and the sound of the golden horse was light and caressing. The stranger led them, and soon they began to see groups of unimaginably marvellous trees, clear groups of trees buried in a dark-blue radiance. And angels were singing in the trees, with reedlike voices. And the tender, loving, all-good Virgin Mary was coming to greet them, and she seemed more like the older sister than the mother of the golden knight, the Sovereign Master of Souls, Jesus Christ.

SOME DAYS LATER, while wandering about in the mountains, the English army suddenly stumbled on the corpses of its lost comrades. And merry

King Richard's heart clouded over. He called for an Arab physician and questioned him about the death of his famous soldiers, questioned him for a long time. Why had they died?

"The sun killed them," answered the learned man. "But do not be sad for them, O King. Before their death they must have seen wonderful dreams, the kind of dreams that we, the living, are never given to see."

Journey to Ether-Land

I

"No," said the old doctor, "narcotics don't affect everyone the same way. One man will die of a single grain of cocaine, another man will take five grains and be no more affected than if he'd drunk a cup of black coffee. I knew a lady who took chloroform and had dreams, saw really astonishing things. Other people just go to sleep. Oh yes, there are some uniform effects—like the shining seas that opium smokers always see—but generally speaking this is a whole hidden science, one of which we've so far had only suspicions—it's a whole new paleontology, perhaps, or some such thing as that. Now you young people, you know, you could be of service to humanity. You could make yourselves excellent cannon fodder—in the hands, of course, of an experienced investigator. The main thing," and he touched his face with a blue-stained finger, "the main thing—yes, is materials. Materials."

An odd doctor. We'd called him, by pure chance, to stop Inna's hysterics. We could have done it ourselves, of course, but we were just tired of the wet towels and the rumpled pillows, and we felt like letting someone else do it. He walked in sedately, sporting a very decent little grey beard, and took care of Inna immediately, putting some sourish stuff under her nose. And then he took a proffered cup of coffee, sprawled out in a chair, and began to chatter away at us, his nose perhaps more up in the air than his advanced age really permitted. I didn't much care, myself, but Mezentsov, who really cared about manners and all that, was furiously angry. With exaggerated politeness he asked the doctor if perhaps the blue stains on his hands, and also on his suit, were after-smears of just such experiments.

"Oh yes," the doctor answered with an important air, "I've been doing quite a lot of work, lately, on the properties of ether."

"Ah," Mezentsov insisted, "but so far as I know, doctor, ether is a highly volatile liquid, and it would certainly have had time to evaporate long ago, since—," and here he looked at his watch, "we have had the good fortune of your pleasant company, now, for a good two hours."

"But haven't I been telling you, over and over, all this time," the doctor exclaimed impatiently, "that science knows almost nothing about the effects of narcotics on the human organism. Me, I do understand a little of that! And I can assure you, my good young man—," and Mezentsov, who was thirty years old, winced, "that if you purchase a bottle of ether, in any ordinary drug store, you will see something distinctly more surprising than the blue on my hands, which just by the way is absolutely none of your business. For ten cents worth of ether, gentlemen, even that marvellous turkish shawl on the young lady will seem to you like a dirty rag, in comparison with what you will come to know."

He bowed, rather coldly, and I went with him to the door. As I came back I heard Inna, languid and—as always after hysterics—a bit hoarse, scolding Mezentsov, "Why did you treat him like that? He's really a very clever man."

"But I, upon my word," Mezentsov justified himself, "I won't be cannon fodder in the hands of a person who doesn't even know enough to wash himself properly."

"I'm entirely on your side, Inna," I took her part, "and I think it will have to come to something like that, unless we want our dear three-some to fall apart. We've learned Baudelaire by heart; perfumed cigarettes make us sick; and even the mildest flirtation just doesn't get off the ground."

"Ah, isn't that true, dear Grant, isn't that just the way it is," she said, somehow animated, all at once. "You bring some ether over here and we'll all smell it together. And Mezentsov will too—of course."

"It's dangerous," Mezentsov grumbled. "You get circles under your eyes, your hands start shaking . . ."

"And don't your hands shake anyway!" Inna was very angry. "Just try and pick up that glass of water, go ahead. Hah! You don't dare. How can you say they don't shake?"

Mezentsov walked over to the window, his feelings hurt.

"I can't do it tomorrow," I said.

"And I can't," echoed Mezentsov, "the day after tomorrow."

"Good Lord, what bores you are!" Inna exclaimed. "This always being busy, busy, isn't at all refined. You're not clerks, after all! Now you listen: this is my final word. Saturday, at eight sharp—and don't argue, I'm not listening to you anyway. You be here with three bottles of ether. If something comes of it—good. And if nothing, then we'll go somewhere. Remember: Saturday! And now, go home; I have to change."

2

Mezentsov came by, Saturday, to go out to dinner with me. We liked quiet dinners like that, sometimes, with just one bottle of wine, and moralizing talk, and sentimental recollections. It was especially pleasant, after a dinner like that, to go back to work at our usual (but not always terribly proper) nothingnesses.

We were sitting in a restaurant, this time, exchanging impressions of Inna and being drowned out by the orchestra. I had been introduced to her about two months before, and I'd soon after taken Mezentsov to her place. She was perhaps twenty years old, and lived alone in one large, very large room, which she rented from a quiet and utterly faceless family. She was fairly well educated, she seemed to have money, she'd lived abroad, and her last name wasn't Russian. As far as externals were concerned, that was really all we knew about her. But we agreed that neither of us had ever met a cleverer, a more beautiful, or a more liberated—and capricious!—girl than Inna. And Mezentsov swore that she was a virgin: he knew how to trace a woman's past by the way she walked, the look in her eyes, by the corners of her mouth. He considered himself a connoisseur in these matters, and he had good reason to, and so I believed him.

Toward the end of our dinner we decided that inhaling ether was just too stupid, and that it would be much better to take Inna skating. So at eight-thirty we drove up to her house, bringing a huge paper kite that Mezentsov had bought from a wandering peddler. We hoped that this present would console Inna for our not having brought ether.

But once in her room, we stopped, amazed. It had been completely transformed. All the little trinkets, all the plates hanging on the walls, everything so dear and so usual, had been hidden, and her bed, and the table, and the couch were all covered with multicolored oriental kerchieves, mixed here and there with old-fashioned colored brocade. (Mezentsov later confided to me that the decorations had made him think of someone getting ready for an exhibit of porcelains or enamels. But they were fine fabrics, and the colors had been chosen with real taste.)

But Inna herself was the most amazing thing of all. She was standing in the middle of the room, wearing a real silk dress of exactly the kind worn by Indian dancing girls, temple whores, a dress with two round insets for her breasts. Her legs were bare, below the knees, and she wore wide shoes that had no backs. Between the tunic part of the dress and the flaring trousers, below, a white strip of her belly showed; her slender faintly dark arms were entwined with thick bronze bracelets. She was sucking on sugar soaked in eau de cologne, to make her eyes bigger and brighter. I was confused, even embarrassed, I admit it, though I had seen dancing girls in the temples of Benares and Delhi.

Mezentsov was smiling faintly and trying to shove his paper kite into a crack somewhere. And we knew that there was no chance of going skating; there were three large, cut glass bottles of ether waiting on the table.

"Good evening, gentlemen," Inna said, not bothering to stretch out her hand to us. "The bright god of wonderful journeys has been waiting. Take your bottles, take your places, and let's begin."

Mezentsov's smile was wry, now, but he did not speak. I stared at the ceiling.

"Well?" said Inna just as seriously. She lay down on the couch, alone, a bottle in her hands. "What's wrong, gentlemen?"

"How are you supposed to inhale the stuff?" Mezentsov asked, seating himself, reluctantly, in a large armchair.

And seeing that it was inevitable, that we would have to sniff it, I wanted to get it over with. I remembered what an ether-addict friend had told me. "Press one nostril to the neck of the bottle," I explained. "You breathe with that. Press the other nostril closed. And don't breathe through your mouth at all: it has to get into your lungs." And uncorking my bottle, I set them an example.

Inna gave me a long, grateful look, and we all became very silent.

After a few minutes, strangely languorous, I heard Mezentsov's metallic voice, "I feel as though I'm floating."

No one answered him.

3

My eyes were closed, I felt an inexpressible lassitude, I had flown millions of miles—but, strangely, deep inside myself. The infinity that had surrounded me, before, fell away, darkened and was gone, but in its place I saw a new one, shining within me. The ugly equilibrium of centrifugal and centripetal, inside the spirit, was turned upside down, and just as a skylark once it has folded its wings drops straight to the earth, so the golden dot of consciousness drops farther and farther inside, and never stops falling, never can stop, never. You see unknown countries. Silhouettes float by, like Chinese shadows: back out on earth they would be called unicorns, and temples, and grass. And when a sudden sweet choking takes your breath away, a quiet push turns me on my back, and I rock, slowly, regularly, on fibrous green and red clouds. Fantastic clouds! Above me, below me, thick, and with open spaces visible through them, white, very white spaces. And the choking returns, and there's another soft push, but this time I'm already soaring off on an infinite flight, down, down, close to the radiant center. The outlines of the clouds change, now, fly up like the clothes of people dancing, it's all a madness of red and green clouds.

A sea—there's a sea all around me, ginger red, foaming and splashing. And on the crests of all of the waves I see a blue foam. Maybe that's what the doctor had all over his hands and his clothes?

I drift to the west. Dolphins are splashing, and sea gulls cutting the waves with their wings, but the bitter water keeps sweeping up over me, and I am about to go under. And then, choking, I felt my nose bleeding, and I was refreshed. But the blood was blue too, like the sea foam, and again I remembered the doctor.

A huge billow threw me out of the water, up onto silver sand, and I guessed that these were the Islands of Absolute Happiness. There were five of them, lying out in the middle of the sea like sleeping camels, and I tried to imagine which were the long necks, and which the small heads, which the familiar curve of the hind legs. I was running under lush palm trees, fanning out green over my head, and I was throwing seashells and laughing. This was the way it had always been, this was the way it would always be. And yet I knew that there would be something completely different. I turned in a new direction,

and there, on a broad white rock stood Inna, naked, her arms and her legs and her shoulders and her hair covered with heavy jewelry, set in such perfect symmetry that they seemed to be held in place only by her wild, terrible beauty. Her cheeks were rose red, her lips were parted like someone catching their breath, her darkened eyes had an extraordinary glow.

"Come up here, Grant," she called, her voice transparent, as yellow as honey. "Come to me. Can't you see that I'm alive?"

I went to her and, stretching out my hand, touched her small, firm, elongated breast.

"I'm alive, I'm alive," she said over and over, and out of the words I felt, blowing, a terrible, lovely scent of earth-grass sinking into bottomlessness.

And suddenly her arms were around my neck, and I felt the gentle heat of her breast and the noisy loveliness of her hot face, bent close to mine.

"Carry me away," she was saying. "Carry me away. After all, you're alive too."

I grabbed her and I ran. She pushed herself against me, urged me on.

"Faster, faster!"

I fell, it was a clearing covered with white sand, pine needles rose all around me, like a wall. I kissed Inna's mouth. She stayed silent, but her eyes were laughing. Then I kissed her again . . .

and how long we were there I don't know. But nowhere, not in any sheik's seraglio, not in any Japanese tea house, have there ever been as many teasing, ravishing caresses. Sometimes we lost consciousness, lost ourselves, lost each other; and a hermaphrodite who looked like a huge Byzantine angel told us about his most recent happiness and yearned to share it, as a woman thirsts for sorrow. And then suddenly, the sweet investigation of each other would begin again.

Some great planet curved in toward the glade, and then swept by. It seemed to be a sign and so, embracing, we too hurried upward. And again there were red and green clouds, and we rode on their arching spines, and again we heard the harsh, foul voices of universal merrymaking. Off to one side, pale, his eyes closed, Mezentsov was rising too, his parchment forehead entwined with flush-red roses. I knew he was muttering incantations and practicing sorcery, though he neither raised his hands nor opened his lips. But this—what was this? There are no more red and green clouds, we're in the middle of a white world, and there are misty, shapeless figures no one has ever seen before. We've lost our way: instead of flying up, out toward the outer world, we went the other way, we descended down into the unknown. I glanced at Inna. She was pale but silent, she still hadn't noticed.

4

It was like an ancient theater, or a large auditorium at the Sorbonne. Silent figures bundled up in white were crowded together, in a semi-circle all around the vast amphitheater. And we were with them, and Mezentsov's roses and Inna's jewelry stood out sharply, against the general whiteness.

And there, there where there should have been a rostrum, or actors, I saw the old doctor. In his elegant, black dress coat he looked like a real lecturer, and he moved about like someone who knew perfectly well how to control his audience. He was obviously just about to start. And my heart contracted, as if something immensely dangerous was about to happen, and I wanted to cry out, but it was too late. I heard his firm, even voice suddenly filling that entire space, "Ladies and gentlemen! The best way to understand each other is to be completely, utterly sincere. If I needed to, I would cheerfully mislead you. But I don't need to. The better, the more clearly you understand where you stand, the better for me. I'll even scare you, I'll tempt you. And my absolute truthfulness will prepare you to withstand any temptation. You are now, ladies and gentlemen, in my country: I offer you the privilege of staying here forever. Consider! You can give up both love and hate, you can forget the alternation of day and night. If you have children, you will give up your children. If you enjoy fame, you will give up your fame. Are you strong enough to give up so much?

"I hide nothing from you. You've barely touched the skin of the fruit, this time, you don't know its real taste. It may seem astringent to you, sour, or too sweet, or too fragrant. And when you bite through to the seed at the center, who knows, perhaps you'll experience the quiet, terrible fragrance of bitter almond? Which of you loves the unknown, which of you wants every tomorrow to be as virginal as a bride, never insulted even in a daydream?

"I call to myself only spirits like electric waves, only gay devourers of space. Here they will find an immeasurability truly worthy of them. Here everything is born for the first time, here everything is unlike anything else. No death interrupts your joy, here, breaks into your movement or knowledge or the long feasting of your eyes. Everything here is your own—because, ladies and gentlemen, everything here—is you, yourselves! But quick, it's growing late, the time is coming: break your ether bottles, or you live here in my country forever!"

He finished, he bowed. A storm of enthusiastic rapture rocked the audience. White sleeves waved in the air and a deafening murmur rose, "The doctor! The doctor! Encore, encore!"

I had never thought Inna's face could light up with such speechless joy, such trembling, palpitating admiration. I couldn't see Mezentsov, though I kept trying to find him in the crowd. But the shouts kept getting louder, and I was beginning to feel vaguely troubled. My legs began to feel heavy, somehow, and I began to notice that I was breathing with difficulty. And then, suddenly, right into my ear, I heard Mezentsov's anxious voice shouting for the doctor, and I opened my eyes.

5

My ether bottle was almost empty. I felt as if I had been thrown back into this familiar room—it was already familiar, I knew where I was, I knew the oriental fabrics and the brocades.

"Don't you see what's happened to Inna? She's dying, she's dying!" Mezentsov was shouting, bending over the couch.

I ran up. She was lying there, not breathing, her half-opened lips turned white, and a thin blue vein bulging from her forehead. "Well," I mumbled, "take the ether bottle away from her," and then I quickly jerked it away myself. She shuddered, her face twisted in pain and, without opening her eyes, burying her face in the pillow, she suddenly began to sob, like a child that has hurt itself.

"Ah, hysterics! Thank God," said Mezentsov, dipping a towel into a pitcher of water. "Only this time we won't call the doctor, no, once was enough!" He began wetting Inna's forehead; I held her hand. In half an hour we were able to begin discussing things.

I have an especially good grip on the miraculous, I never forget it, I always remember everything in all of my dreams, and so—understandably—I wanted the others to speak first. But Inna was still too weak, and so Mezentsov began, "I saw nothing, but I felt the oddest things. I rocked, and I fell, and I rose up once more, and I completely forgot what was good and what was evil. And that was such fun that I decided to work some evil on someone, except that I didn't know who to do it to, because I saw nobody. I got tired of that, after a while, and then it was no trick to just open my eyes."

And then Inna said, "I don't remember, I don't remember, but oh, if only I could remember! I was in the middle of clouds, and then I was on some kind of sand, and I felt so good. It seems as if I can still feel all the warmth of that happiness. Why did you take my ether away? I should have stayed, I should have gone on."

And I said that I had seen clouds too, red and green clouds, and that I had heard voices and much conversation, but that I could no longer repeat what I'd heard. I wanted to hide what had happened, God only knows why. Inna nodded happily at everything I said. When I was finished, she exclaimed, "Tomorrow we'll do it again. But we need more ether."

"No, Inna, no," I answered. "We wouldn't see a thing, tomorrow. We'd only get a huge headache. I've been warned that ether can only affect an organism that's unprepared for it, so that we'll only see things if we let ourselves get out of the habit."

"And how long will that take?"

"Oh, about three years!"

"You're teasing me," Inna said, angry. "I can wait for a week, well, maybe two, but it will be torture. But three years . . . No. Grant, think of something. You've got to think of something."

"Well," I joked, "go to Ireland, then, where the real ether-addicts are, a whole network of them. They have better methods of inhaling, of course, and I suspect their ether is purer, too. But they die off too fast, or else they'd be the happiest of people."

Inna was silent, thoughtful. Mezentsov rose, and I left with him. We were silent too. An unpleasant smell of ether lined our mouths; a cigarette tasted bitter.

When we went back to Inna's, we were told that she had gone, and they gave us a note, addressed to me.

Thank you for your advice, dear Grant! I'm going to Ireland. I hope I find there what I've spent my whole life searching for. My regards to Mezentsov.

> *Your,*
> *Inna.*
> *P.S. Why did you take the*
> *ether away from me, that time?*

Mezentsov read her note too, and for a while was silent. Then he said, more quietly than usual, "Did you notice how strangely Inna's eyes, and her lips, changed after the ether? You'd think she'd had a lover."

I shrugged, understanding that the most wilful, the most beautiful girl had just walked out of my life, forever.

Drama

The Poisoned Tunic

A TRAGEDY IN FIVE ACTS

DRAMATIS PERSONAE
Imru, *an Arab Poet*
Justinian, *Emperor of Byzantium*
Theodora, *Empress of Byzantium*
Zoe, *Justinian's Daughter*
The King of Trapezond, *Zoe's Suitor*
A Eunuch, *Justinian's Confidant*

The time is the beginning of the sixth century after Christ. The place is a hall in the Constantinople palace. The action occurs over a time span of twenty-four hours; night falls between Act III and Act IV.

ACT I

Scene i. Imru *and the* Eunuch

EUNUCH: You're Imru, the Bedouin: yes? I've heard
of your people. Our king
does not rule in your lands,
you do not rest in Justinian's golden hands,
but I've heard of your people, yes,
and I will hear what you say. Speak.

IMRU: Sir, treachery and evil—that's all
my early days have been full of.
I was born, east of Yemen,
son of Gohdzir, a Bedouin king.
But my father's people loved me, and my father was
   afraid,
and I ran, and
for years I ate alien bread, drank alien water,
whispered greetings in front of alien tents.
I became a poet so that
sheiks and emirs and mullahs would caress my soul.
My songs flew like Roman eagles
across the land. And somehow,
one night, at a singing contest,
the Benu-Assad poet
—how I hate that name!—

sang, and as he sang he stared at me,
"Gohdzir the Bedouin king was a mighty warrior:
ah, how bitter are his wife's tears . . ."
I knew at once, I killed him
on the spot and whipped
my camel homeward,
eight days at full speed and
then
I saw: no towers, only a pile of rocks,
bits of torn hide in the sheepfold.
And like a wounded bird
I came straight to Constantinople.
I said to myself, "The Emperor might help,
somehow the Emperor might help."
And what I want to ask him for
is six thousand spears
and four thousand bows
and two thousand swords, trained swords,
and pack-loads for them all.
That is what I want to ask.

EUNUCH: Why should the emperor bother
with the empty struggles of alien people?
What can he win, what glory can he find
in such petty wars?

IMRU: When the slimy Benu-Assad
have what the Benu-Assad deserve
my country will be eternally grateful and
loyal to the emperor forever. I swear it.

EUNUCH: I can't predict what the emperor
will say; these conquests are often
unstable, sometimes
difficult, and always
unnecessary. But I will tell him. You've heard,
perhaps, that we've started to turn
the vast disorder of the emperor's
laws into one clear and orderly code
of all the law. No one will need
to fear a poison tongue, soon, or evil lies. And so
what good are conquests
to us? But still, I'll tell him. But first,

the truth: are you a Manichean? Are you?
What are your views of the Incarnation, eh?

IMRU: There's no time to think about God, in the desert.
We have war, and lions, and the shifting sand.
But once, along the road, I saw
old people praying to a black rock.

EUNUCH: Well, that's fine, that's nothing! A pagan
we can baptize, after all, but only iron
can help a heretic.
You know: to win a war there must be a general,
someone who knows foot soldiers and horsemen,
someone who knows the people and the desert too,
someone who quietly obeys the emperor's every word.
And what if we chose you?

IMRU: I was a reckless wanderer, and I heard
how my father had been killed, and
now I always hear a marvellous voice
telling me tales of vengeance.
And if this voice spoke in a crowd
its flame would drown the sound, it would silence the
    sounds
of war, as if it came from the throat of a creature
dressed in armor and wearing leopard fur.
I swore to use no perfume,
to eat nothing that was not stale, to drink no wine,
and not to touch a woman
until my wrong was avenged.

EUNUCH: But why did you come to Byzantium,
you funny savage? Our perfumes
come from musk, from rose oil,
from ambergris and crushed gillyflowers,
and you won't find their like among the Eskimos
or the deadly Sumatrans and Javanese.
When we feast we eat
bulls, stuffed with honey and olives;
and small pigeons, tender pigeons,
tasty, ah tasty, like the bliss of paradise.
And we wash them down with sacred wine,
thousands of years in its casks: all that's left
is pure and strong and fragrant,

and black, and thick like tar.
And women! I can say no more:
as a priest my tongue is stopped.
But this I can say: keep your word, if you can,
prove we can trust you,
and then we'll send you to Arabia, oh yes,
and to India, too, even
to great and glorious China.
                    [*Exit the* Eunuch. *Enter* Zoe]

Scene ii. Imru *and* Zoe

ZOE: Aren't you my new teacher,
            just come from the South, come to teach me
            didactics and the magic of grasses and herbs?

IMRU: No, young lady, not me. I could teach you
            other things:
            crawling up to an enemy's house
            dragging a smoldering torch through the grass—
            or how to leap onto a milk-white camel
            and ride the sands for hours,
            then come to the Bay of Jedda and
            flicking your wrist, so,
            rip the guts out of a sea monster.
            I could teach you careless passion, too,
            and songs about the slow heaviness of lovely eyes,
            and songs about the pleasures of night
            and the dark—but those you've heard,
            of course, and you've sung them too,
            over and over.

ZOE: No, no. All I've heard are masses
            and sermons, I've heard nothing else.
            You're the first in the world
            to tell me about love.

IMRU: You mean . . . no one's ever kissed you?
            There's no one you've ever kissed?

ZOE: I've kissed the smooth stones
            rolled up by the sea,
            I've kissed jasmine petals

blossoming under my window.
When the pain was too great
I've kissed my hands, and my arms,
but no one has kissed me,
not since my mother died.

IMRU: But—how old are you?

ZOE: I'm past thirteen.

IMRU: Girls your age are married, where I come from,
or else they have lovers. I remember,
oh I remember, one girl . . .

ZOE: Tell me, please tell me!

IMRU: The stars were full of fire,
like the diamonds in a woman's dress,
and her brothers were hunting me, up and down,
like desert wolves, their knives drawn.
But I crept through, like a serpent
I came to her. She was ready
for bed, her clothes all taken off, and she said,
"Go back: you won't have me.
Why won't you meet me where people can see?"
But she came with me, she came.
We pulled a colored cloth behind us, to wipe
our footsteps out of the sand.
We came to the place where the white
lily cups rose up out of the water,
and I put my hands around her head
and she wound her arms around my waist—
and how hot her mouth was!
Only mirrors shine like her breasts.
Her eyes were as shy as a gazelle
standing guard over its calf,
and that musky fragrance in my bed—
I still smell that scent, it will never fade.
—What's wrong? What's the matter? Why are you
crying?

ZOE: Leave me alone. No: no one's ever told me
that my eyes were like a gazelle's,
that my mouth is hot,
that only mirrors shine like my breasts!

IMRU: From the day I came to manhood, I swear it,
           I've met no one like you,
           I've never seen beauty so innocent,
           so triumphant.
           I've sworn not to touch a woman: I have no choice.
           But you've burned into my fate,
           I must have you, I will.
           I'll be revenged, and then I'll return. For you.

ZOE: You don't know who I am.

IMRU: Wait: don't go.
           Suppose you're a Roman, I'm only a simple Arab,
           but that's nothing. Or maybe your father
           is too noble? Perhaps he's a captain, a general?
           In that case—

ZOE: My name is Zoe. My father is Justinian.
                    [Imru *releases her. Exit* Zoe. *Enter* Theodora]

Scene iii. Imru *and* Theodora

THEODORA: How lovely that was! Fine. Now I know
           why you came to Constantinople,
           you lyric poet, you terrible avenger,
           who swears arrogant oaths.
           We're supposed to give you everything,
           soldiers and girls.
           Well: what do you have to say? Answer me! You had
           no trouble talking to my stepdaughter, just now.

IMRU: And walls have ears, here. Children
           know that, but I had forgotten,
           and I'm silent, now, because
           perhaps I've already talked too much.

THEODORA: How pointless, poet! I'm no enemy—I'll even tell you
           some amusing news.
           Zoe has just been promised
           to the king of Trapezond. By me.
           In marriage. Aren't you happy?

IMRU: Lady, I'm neither merry nor sad.
           Is a Bedouin to dream
           of the emperor's daughter?

THEODORA: Perhaps you swore
            only what was suddenly fact, not simply words.
            Perhaps you're no longer a man,
            your body no longer needs a woman's caresses.

IMRU: When I think of women, suddenly,
            I smother, I choke,
            my eyes go dark, I hear a misty beating
            in my ears, my heart slows down, beats like a distant
                drum.

THEODORA: But how silly you are! The king of Trapezond
            is a famous general, to be sure,
            and a wise ruler,
            and a tender lover;
            but with Zoe he's always terribly shy,
            as if he were the bride, not her.
            And girls—I know you know it,
            I've heard your song—girls want
            something very different.

IMRU: Are you saying, lady—can you possibly be saying—
            that I could have the princess Zoe for my wife?

THEODORA: Well, no, not for your wife. Who are you, compared to
                her?
            But you can have her!
            And I suspect I might help you.
            This palace has more than a few rooms, empty,
            soft with Bokhara rugs, and Smyrna rugs,
            and the palace gardens have more than a few thick
                soft lawns,
            and a wall to keep other eyes out.
            And you're hungry for a woman,
            and your slender waist, your smooth
            arms, your melodious voice and those splendid images
            you speak in are exactly what a girl's heart wants—and
            well, what do you say? Is it a bargain?

IMRU: Lady, I see
            how well you test my honesty.

THEODORA: I knew it: you didn't believe a word.
            But I need you, poet, and I'll tell you
            why I've made these plans.
            I hit her with a whip, once,

and that proud little bitch
went pale, and stood there all arrogant
and called me—me, the empress of Byzantium
—and with maidservants listening
—a street whore out of Alexandria. Me!
I did not ascend this throne
to pardon insults of that sort.
So let her be the whore,
let the king of Trapezond
refuse his disgraced bride!

IMRU: Lady, forgive me. My songs
have caught girls' hearts,
but my love brings them
peace and joy, not sorrow, not shame.

THEODORA: Yes, your passion fizzles and foams
like new wine, but nothing comes of it.
But we'll wait, and it will turn silent
and very strong, like wine in casks, deep in cellars.
And in the meantime, remember, poet: when
the king of Trapezond returns to Constantinople
he'll marry Zoe,
and he will be the one to untie her virgin belt,
he'll bare her breasts,
he'll touch her knees with burning lips . . .
and you? You'll wander up and down these corridors,
    alone,
a long-faced, dull beggar for spears and swords.
                    [*Exit* Theodora. *Enter* Trapezond]

Scene iv. Imru *and* Trapezond

TRAPEZOND: Have you seen the Princess Zoe?
Hasn't the Princess Zoe been here?

IMRU: I've known this palace for a single day,
I don't even know your name,
my noble lord.

TRAPEZOND: I'm the king of Trapezond.
You seem surprised.

IMRU: I haven't seen the princess.

TRAPEZOND:	Praised be Mary! No one can fathom
	the human heart: when I'm far from my belovèd
	I feel that it would be worth death itself
	to hear her walking, to hear her dress rustle
	—but when it comes time to see her
	I rejoice at every delay.

IMRU:	[*To himself*] So: these are those happy arms,
	big, strong, a hero's—
	here they are, those parched lips,
	lit up with laughter as if with the sun.
	Him, it's about him that the empress whispered!

TRAPEZOND:	And why are you here, friend? I've never understood
	what brings you all to Byzantium—
	from the sea, from broad deserts, to these
	dismal, alien palaces!
	Except for Zoe, do you think I'd leave
	my small, my incomparable city
	with its wonderful crisscrossed net of streets, narrow
	streets
	running from shore to shore, and
	its one great square where often
	I sit and hand out justice
	beneath the shade of a hundred-year-old tree?
	Why are you here? Tell me.

IMRU:	Because my father's been killed!
	I want revenge, and I think the emperor
	will give me soldiers.

TRAPEZOND:	Now that's a man talking!
	I love the ringing of steel,
	and the blood bright in your face
	and running hot in your veins.
	Your hand: I'll help you.

IMRU:	No. We southerners
	aren't Byzantines, we don't know how to lie,
	we think it's shameful to steal
	from a friend, sinful to take what's his.

TRAPEZOND:	But what could you be taking from me?
	After all, I'm hardly the emperor of Byzantium,
	my treasury hasn't

any gold, any rare mosaics,
only my father's armor
and some old clothes my mother wore, and wore out,
and the cross our apostle Paul used
to make Christians of my people.
Or were you thinking about my city?
When I was born, friend, the people
feasted with my father, feasted for a week.
When I was a child I played with their children.
They'd all side with their king,
fight tooth and claw.
What else have I got? Fame, that's all, glory.
I'd be glad to share it with you!
When you sink painted Russian boats, as I do,
out on the roaring Pontus,
when you climb a black precipice, deep in the
    Caucasus,
and tackle a wild ox with only a spear in your hand
—then you'll be my equal!
I have spoken.
              [*Enter the* Eunuch]

Scene v. *The* Eunuch *and* Justinian

EUNUCH: The emperor.
                        [*Exeunt* Imru *and* Trapezond. *Enter* Justinian]

JUSTINIAN: Have the ambassadors returned from Rome?

EUNUCH: Yesterday, O Born-to-the-Royal-Purple.

JUSTINIAN: Did they deliver the letter?

EUNUCH: They were not well received.

JUSTINIAN: I knew it! Rome, Rome, so
               proud of her pagan glory:
               she refuses to understand that now
               the world's sun is Constantinople, and only
               Constantinople. But Saint Sophia's:
               how is my cathedral coming?

EUNUCH: Another column was put up, today,
               and the master builder heard angels
               singing happily.

JUSTINIAN:	Give them another five hundred pieces of gold!
	Oh Lord, Lord:
	will I ever enter this temple, see it finished,
	and on my knees
	as Your poor, neglectful servant, give You
	my accounts, all I have done, all I have failed to do?
	By Your divine power
	You commanded me to this royal labor, telling me
	how the world will become a temple, and above it, poised
	like a bell tower, the power of this empire
	crowned with Your cross, O Lord—
	and shall I betray You, in that great hour?
	[*Turning to the* Eunuch] Why isn't the tunic ready?
EUNUCH:	For the king of Trapezond?
JUSTINIAN:	Of course!
EUNUCH:	The gold crown needs to be embroidered—but
	believe me, no king has ever worn
	a tunic so beautiful.
JUSTINIAN:	It must be soaked in poison for three days.
	Are you sure you know the method?
EUNUCH:	Your majesty!
JUSTINIAN:	Well, what is it?
EUNUCH:	I don't understand. Does this mean
	there will be no wedding?
JUSTINIAN:	What makes you think that?
EUNUCH:	But—the bride's sorrow?
JUSTINIAN:	What are a girl's tears
	compared to the needs of the empire? Trapezond
	is a coastal city, it does a superb trade,
	it is the key to the Caucasus, and
	it must be mine.
	I have no fondness for war when bloodless methods
	can be used.
	Let Zoe inherit the city:
	I will rule it, at her request,
	and another priceless pearl
	will grace the crown of Byzantium.
EUNUCH:	I understand, your majesty! You are wise, you are good.

ACT II

Scene i. Justinian, Trapezond, *and the* Eunuch

JUSTINIAN: Dear son, you have come to us again,
from your faraway wars.
The empress will be delighted,
and someone else will be still happier.

TRAPEZOND: Your majesty, how can I thank you
for these gracious but puzzling words?
Sir, your enemies have been defeated,
the Bulgarians have run into their hills, to hide from
    your might.

JUSTINIAN: Yes, of course.

TRAPEZOND: But you can't have known.
I am the first in all the army to arrive.

JUSTINIAN: Why, you were there, my son, and what more is there
    to say?
Your lips have never brought us
news of anything but victory.

EUNUCH: And such an important victory,
so quick a victory,
freeing our legions for other affairs—
O Born-to-the-Royal-Purple, this news will change
many things. News is only news when it is reported.

JUSTINIAN: Then begin. And you, dear son,
listen carefully. You have been the hand holding
our strong sword, but the day will come
when you will be the head
that wears this imperial crown.
[*To the* Eunuch] I'm listening.

EUNUCH: A wanderer has come from the south,
from Arabia, where brother has lifted his sword
against brother, and son against father,
and all is discord. This wanderer swears
that with ten or twelve thousand
imperial soldiers

he can put his murder-weary land
at your feet.

JUSTINIAN: My dear son, what do you say?

TRAPEZOND: I've seen the man. I like
his hawk's face and eyes,
his strong chest, like a copper shield.
He spoke to me strangely, but that
I forgive. My father—
if I may be permitted to so address you—
send your soldiers to Arabia,
let him be their general,
let him build, where his burned home
once stood, a tall city
with fountains, with gardens and palaces.
Oh, I am happy today: I want
others to be happy too.

JUSTINIAN: Ah, I see that young men in love
should not decide matters of state.
Perhaps this wanderer could lead
an army, win a war,
glorify our imperial name,
yes—but tell me this. Who can assure me
that having won his war his blood won't run hot
—the blood of a savage, mind you,
a savage who loves his freedom
and considers slavery a loathsome thing—
and that, then, using our power,
he won't turn victory to his own use?
No, my son, our Byzantine soldiers
deserve another leader, a better leader.
You will be our general, my eternal conqueror,
husband of my beloved daughter, Zoe.
Your wedding is tomorrow: you will take
your young queen with you—and my present
to you, a tunic fit for a king, for an emperor,
will be finished and waiting
when you return.

EUNUCH: The wanderer wants more than victory, he wants
revenge.
If we forget him, he could prove dangerous.

JUSTINIAN: In which case he stays here,
               a hostage under guard, to protect the state
               against unsuspected treachery.
                         [*Exeunt* Justinian *and the* Eunuch. *Enter* Zoe]

Scene ii. Trapezond *and* Zoe

TRAPEZOND: Princess, I'm told you were willing
               to see me—but perhaps
               they were in error? I'll leave you . . .

ZOE: Stay!

TRAPEZOND: [*Looking out the palace window*]
               The wind has whipped the sea into mounds,
               the Bosphorus is white, all white. How I'd love
               to ride away, now!

ZOE: Where?

TRAPEZOND: I don't know! I've never seen that land
               where—like a clear-singing bird, like a rose bush
               —happiness, unknown happiness, just comes flashing
                   by.
               I've watched for it, alongside every crossroad,
               behind every little cloud that ran out onto the sky,
               and all I've seen is bald, insolent mountains
               and clear, unfeeling stars.
               But I know—oh, I know it, I know it!—
               that there are such places,
               and that you don't walk there, you dance,
               and love is sweet and not painful.

ZOE: Is love really painful?

TRAPEZOND: Yes.

ZOE: But what if the stars are full of fire,
               like the diamonds in a woman's dress?
               But what if white lily cups rise
               out of the water, like visions?

TRAPEZOND: I don't understand what you're saying.

ZOE: Neither do I—I . . . dreamed that.

TRAPEZOND:	Zoe! Let's go away, Zoe, I can't breathe here!
	People frown, here, they always want something,
	they don't just talk about love, they want
	to talk about other things.
	And your eyes must hurt, too,
	seeing nothing but jasper walls,
	and your feet must be chilled by these marble floors.
ZOE:	But do you know how to ride a camel?
	Do you know how to kill sea monsters?
	Can you come to me, like a serpent,
	when my brothers are hunting you, up and down, like
	wolves?
TRAPEZOND:	You haven't any brothers.
ZOE:	But will you tell me
	that my eyes are like a gazelle's,
	that my mouth is hot, that only mirrors
	shine like my breasts?
TRAPEZOND:	That Arab! Zoe, tell me, have you seen the Arab?
	A gloomy-faced stranger: did he speak to you?
	Yes, yes: it could only have been him,
	teaching you such words!
	And now you're trembling like a caged bird
	and there is death in my soul. Zoe, oh Zoe,
	please, please: tell me the truth,
	tell me he didn't talk to you!
ZOE:	I don't know, I don't know who I talked to.
	He was tall, like a vision,
	his eyes gleamed like stars,
	his lips were red like roses,
	his words were like a heart beating.
TRAPEZOND:	But his feet didn't touch the ground, did they?
	There were wings, folded and trembling behind his
	back:
	weren't there?
ZOE:	I think so.
TRAPEZOND:	Ah, so it was an angel who came to you!
	But of course: you're a saint, Zoe, a holy saint,
	and of course they come to you from Heaven.
	How pale you are. I can't stand

	seeing you like that. Hurry back to your room
	and rest, there with your prayer-books
	and flowers, and with angels around you, there
	on your pure bed. But first:
	forgive me, Zoe.
ZOE:	There is nothing for me to forgive.

[*Exit* Zoe. *Enter* Theodora]

Scene iii. Trapezond *and* Theodora

THEODORA:	Empress!
THEODORA:	I was looking for Zoe.
	Didn't I hear you talking to her?
TRAPEZOND:	Our talk tired her:
	she's just now left.
THEODORA:	Ah: you're not even married, and already you
	can exhaust the bride. You're an incomparable lover!
	And what were you and Zoe talking about? Tell me.
TRAPEZOND:	Forgive me, Empress, but to hear that name
	which makes the heart beat fast
	from lips which don't realize all the wonder
	that's in it—that hurts me.
THEODORA:	That's not at all fair. I love
	Zoe, as I love you, with a tender love.
TRAPEZOND:	I do not feel it,
	and neither does Zoe. Have you ever spoken to me
	about her loveliness—once?—about the sweet bliss
	of her honest eyes and her brave lips,
	about the heavenly angels who descend to her?
THEODORA:	Tell me: has the emperor set
	the day for your wedding?
TRAPEZOND:	It will be tomorrow.
THEODORA:	Well, my congratulations!
	And as for angels—no, I really haven't heard
	about any angels coming to her.
	And those others—well, you're about to be married,
	so why bother to discuss such things?

TRAPEZOND: Empress: you could not confuse Princess Zoe,
nor can you confuse a heart full of love for her,
with talk of that sort.

THEODORA: Confuse you? But is there something evil
about Zoe meeting an Arab
and hearing him warble melodious nonsense?

TRAPEZOND: Meeting an Arab?

THEODORA: Yes. And he sang so sweetly in her ear,
all about sea monsters, and camels,
and of course all about his own amorous adventures,
of which I gather there have been many.
And I think, if I remember it right, he asked to kiss her
—but of course Zoe said no and wouldn't allow it.

TRAPEZOND: The Arab: she lied to me!

THEODORA: Oh, such jealousy! Just think: he's only a wanderer,
a miserable beggar, really, and you, you're a king.
It is true that he's handsome, though, rather handsomer
than you, and he can upset a young girl's heart
with well-woven speeches; he can come to her, at night,
in her dreams, shining like a golden angel,
and make her weep and grow pale with passion
—but a wise girl, a sensible girl,
would hardly fall in love with some unknown stranger.

TRAPEZOND: Leave me, Empress: please. You have hurt me
too much. I believe in Zoe,
I would die if I could not believe in her.
But that Arab will know
what my vengeance means.
He would have been better unborn—

THEODORA: [*Interrupting him*]
And here he is! Proceed, proceed with your vengeance!
[*Enter* Imru]

Scene iv. Trapezond, Theodora, *and* Imru

IMRU: You're here: hah! Tell me the truth:
are you to be the general, in my place?

The eunuch told me the whole thing. How could you
    dare!
You've stolen the very last joy I had in the world!

TRAPEZOND: You talked to Zoe, secretly,
and told me you'd not even seen her!
You were a tiger, I thought—I see, now, you're a hyena
covered with a tiger's striped hide.

IMRU: You're a miserable thief, but you dare to preach
at me. A thief who stole his crust of bread
from a starving beggar. Do you think I can just sur-
    render
that sacred vengeance, wrung out of heaven?

TRAPEZOND: Your dirty lips whispered
dirty words to the Princess Zoe,
and your insolent eyes dared to look into
hers, which are as pure as paradise.

IMRU: Oh, miserable country, miserable Arabia!
Can I have done this to you, I?
I meant to heal your wounds—
but him, a stranger, what will he do to you?

TRAPEZOND: I will burn your country to the ground,
I will fill the wells with sand,
I will tear down every wall,
I will cut the trees around the oases,
and no one will know that such a country existed,
its very name will die!
And you, Arab, you are going to rot in chains, in a
    dungeon,
and even when your hair is white and you are old and
tottering, you will rot there.
And you'll bless me, after a while,
for the stale crust of bread they throw down to you,
once a week.
> [Imru *draws his knife and attacks*
> Trapezond. *After a struggle,* Trapezond
> *forces* Imru *down and takes away the knife*]

IMRU: Kill me, kill me!

TRAPEZOND: Kill you?
I wouldn't dirty my hands with such blood.
I kill only worthy men.

THEODORA: The commandment tells us not to avenge ourselves
             upon those who have injured us: remember, King,
             you're a Christian.

TRAPEZOND: Yes—but it will be exactly as I have said.
             He will be taken tonight, thrown into chains.
             His kind should not walk free
             where the sun shines, where noble things
             are done, and where girls
             like my Zoe walk by.

ACT III

Scene i. Justinian *and* Theodora

THEODORA: My beloved, my Emperor: so tomorrow
             the king of Trapezond and the Princess Zoe
             are to be married, and the avenging Arab
             is to have chains, not soldiers?
             I'm glad. But it hurts me when
             I hear your decisions
             not from your calm, stern lips
             that I have kissed so well in the lonely darkness,
             but from your eunuch, from your advisors,
             even from blabbing, empty-headed servants.

JUSTINIAN: How long I tried to govern
             with you at my side—
             how I trusted, how I loved you—
             and how cruelly, in the end, you deceived me!
             You're not my wife, you're only a woman.
             Perhaps others forget but I,
             I forget nothing.

THEODORA: Again—once again you repeat
             these fables that no one believes, not now.
             My father was a senator: your guardian of the seal
             has the documents. Anyone who calls them forged
             speaks nonsense. And they prove everything.

JUSTINIAN: I don't need to know who your father was:
             I'm your husband, I need no other authority!
             Haven't you guessed what I mean?

THEODORA: All women are alike.

JUSTINIAN: No, not all women!
               Zoe's mother, like a lily of the Lord,
               shone with heavenly purity—
               and Zoe is like her.

THEODORA: The Arab
               goes to prison?

JUSTINIAN: Yes.

THEODORA: Forgive me, forgive me!
               I've been your wife these ten years
               and in ten years there's been nothing, nothing
               you can reproach me for. You're cruel.

JUSTINIAN: You came to my bed unclean.

THEODORA: Yes, unclean! But do you know why?
               Only because I loved you so much,
               my Emperor, my mighty eagle!
               As a little girl I used to dream of you;
               I hid your picture among my clothes.
               When your royal procession wound through the streets
               to the games, no one could have torn me from the
                   window.
               I bribed one of your slaves, once,
               to bring me sand from the garden
               where you walked, alone, in the evenings,
               meditating on the good of Byzantium.
               But years passed, and my blood began to glow
               and boil, and finally
               I met a man whose look, whose walk,
               whose voice, everything about him, was exactly
               like you—you . . . It was said
               that one night your father took
               his mother to bed.
               You were far away, a stranger, I could not come to you,
               and he turned pale in my presence, melting with love.
               And I gave myself, but only once, only once,
               I swear it! And soon after he was dead,
               killed fighting with your armies in Illyria.

JUSTINIAN: But you were in Alexandria, later on,
               and there are some rumors about that.

THEODORA: My confessor, Pankraty, sent me

	to Alexandria, to a holy hermit, to pray for forgiveness.
JUSTINIAN:	There's an old saying: if you suspect a woman is lying you can never suspect her enough.
THEODORA:	Then send me away! Take my title from me, now, at once. It means nothing to me, without love. Let it be, again, as it was: I will stand at my window and watch you as you pass through the streets. You've changed, but I'm just as I was, I'm still that little girl who loves you. Beat me, drive me away.
JUSTINIAN:	[*Extending his hand to her*] My child!
THEODORA:	[*Weeping*] How could I love like that if I didn't love you tenderly? You are tender to me, now, as you once were. Shall we forget the quarrels, the jealousy? Let us live for happiness, our own and the state's, granted mysteriously by God. Give me your ring, the ring that makes an emperor of him who wears it, able to give orders and to cancel them, in your name. Give me your ring as a pledge of our reconciliation, as you gave it to me, once, as a pledge of your love, and I will believe, as I want to believe, that we're friends again, really good friends. [*Lowering her voice*] I know everything. I touch your hands and the blood that warms them whispers secrets to me, I lie on your breast and the beating of your heart is as clear as words. I know the king of Trapezond's tunic, his wedding present, will be poisoned, but I say nothing against you, I submit to everything. If you killed the holy Patriarch and glorified the Manichean sin as the true religion of the state, I would follow you everywhere just to be close to you.

JUSTINIAN: [*Giving her the ring*] Child, child.

THEODORA: Now leave me.
                   My soul is filled with such happiness
                   that I must turn to prayer.

JUSTINIAN: I should be glad
                   to pray with you.

THEODORA: Ah, no!
                   A holy Mother Superior is coming to me,
                   and she is forbidden to see or be seen by a man.
                             [*Noises from backstage*]
                   I hear her coming. Hurry, leave me.
                             [*Exit* Justinian. *Enter* Imru, *running and fol-
                             lowed by the* Eunuch]

Scene ii. Theodora, Imru, *and the* Eunuch

IMRU: Lady, your boy told me
                   you were waiting, but this mad old man
                   tried to put me in chains.
                   I killed his soldier—and here I am.
                   This city is rotten with treachery.

EUNUCH: Empress: I do only what the emperor
                   has ordered. Please:
                   go to your rooms so that your eyes
                   need not be offended by the sight of violence.

THEODORA: Wait.
                   [*To* Imru] Have you decided?

IMRU: The price of my freedom is my life.

THEODORA: The king of Trapezond insisted, at the council meeting,
                   that you be put under guard at once.

IMRU: The king of Trapezond! I'll kill him.

THEODORA: You'll kill him? But this isn't the Arabian desert
                   —and, just as important, he's stronger.

EUNUCH: Don't you see, my lady, that this wild beast
                   is dangerous, if left free?
                   Please: let me take him.

THEODORA:	A moment! [*To* Imru] Do wrongs like these wash away in blood?
IMRU:	But what else can they be washed away with?
EUNUCH:	Forgive me, Empress, I must take him.
THEODORA:	This ring: you know what it means. The Arab will not be put in chains: I do not like violence and anger and spite, I will heal his sin-troubled soul with the truths of the Gospel. Leave us.
EUNUCH:	I submit. [*Exit the* Eunuch]

Scene iii. Theodora *and* Imru

THEODORA:	And *now* do you believe me a reliable defender of your interests?
IMRU:	I believe that where there is a lion, there is always A hyena too.
THEODORA:	You may insult me as you please: what is a title to an Arab, what can you know of grandeur?
IMRU:	Lead me, teach me, I'm yours!
THEODORA:	What are you saying?
IMRU:	Zoe: I can't forget her, I think of her all the time, just as a faint red flame flicks out, touches, disappears—but the skin is burned.
THEODORA:	Didn't you know that I was joking? One doesn't seduce an emperor's daughter!
IMRU:	If I must, I will find my way alone. Goodbye!

THEODORA: Wait: do you really think you're going? That's not the
way.
You'll do so many stupid things
that in a hundred years I could not undo them.
Still, I like your passion,
your riotous Arabian blood.
If I were not the empress
I might well fall in love with you myself.

IMRU: Goodbye. Why all these empty words?

THEODORA: For this: perhaps
you should put your dangerous passion aside
and have mercy on Zoe. She's to be a bride,
and she loves her husband.

IMRU: She loves him?

THEODORA: I think they're
close, close. At any rate
she told him
how you'd bragged, how you humbled yourself, later,
and he was angry, and she laughed.

IMRU: Empress, I see your slyness, your cunning:
it's perfectly plain. Lie to other people, please,
to children, to old men in love with you,
to noble idiots, to other liars, and flatterers;
but not to me, a desert-wanderer
who trusts only in clouds,
and in himself, and in a song he knows he's already
sung.
Do you want me to be more passionate? It's a waste.
I burn like a forest fire, I need no whipping up,
I feel like a bowstring
pulled taut by some mighty arm.
My decision has been changed,
it can't be changed again.

THEODORA: I like you, Arab, I really do. I don't need to
hide things, with you, or be cunning.
Your soul is blacker than a starless night,
adored by lovers and by witches . . .
What if I were to fall in love with you?

IMRU: Give me Zoe.

THEODORA: You're right, of course. We both have our vengeance,
             and I'm the empress.
             Now: leave—but stay just behind that door.
             In a moment Zoe will come,
             and I will talk to her like her mother,
             and scold her, and you enter
             when you see me leave.
                        [*Exit* Imru. *Enter* Zoe, *with* Trapezond *be-
                        hind her*]

Scene iv. Theodora, Zoe, *and* Trapezond

THEODORA: Is that you, Zoe?

ZOE: Yes, Empress.

THEODORA: What's this—you, too?

TRAPEZOND: Me, yes. Have we confused you?

THEODORA: No—I'm touched.

TRAPEZOND: This is no time for mocking chatter.
             I feel danger everywhere, now—
             not for myself, but for Princess Zoe.
             I can't afford to leave her for a moment;
             at night I will post myself outside her door,
             sword in hand.

THEODORA: [*To* Zoe] And you consented?

ZOE: Yes.

THEODORA: [*To* Trapezond] What is this danger?

TRAPEZOND: The pure are in danger, everywhere, wherever you are.

THEODORA: You're forgetting yourself:
             I am the empress of Byzantium.

TRAPEZOND: I've forgotten nothing. I know
             that treachery and violence follow you everywhere,
             the secret dagger,
             and poison, and iron heated
             for burning out eyes.
             And the Arab isn't in chains yet, is he?

THEODORA: And how is this Arab any business of yours?

TRAPEZOND:	The echoes in these halls: do you think they speak only to you? You've meant to give the princess to the Arab, you drive him to vengeance, and into passion; you've made him like a tiger that can smell its prey —but Empress, I can conquer both a tiger and a crawling snake.
THEODORA:	So that's your famous kingly blood, your brave heart. And Zoe consents to this? Then what is she? A princess for whom the Lord in heaven has chosen a husband —or a whore, for every passerby to insult and abuse? I had thought she was pure—
TRAPEZOND:	She is, I swear she is—
THEODORA:	Ah: in short, you'll stand in front of her bedroom, sword in hand, the rest of your life, listening, tracking, hiding, one moment believing, the next suspecting. Far-off wars will no longer concern you, there'll be no time to rule your own land. Your days will be more bitter even than wormwood, and your nights will be like the tortures of hell.
TRAPEZOND:	She's pure, I swear it! Zoe: tell her what you think.
ZOE:	I don't know.
THEODORA:	If you humiliate her with this constant suspicion, Zoe may feel herself in a prison— and then, one day, she may say to herself, "Is this really what I'm like?" And then, what happens then—you already know.
TRAPEZOND:	Enough, silence. I could wish, now, that temptations would fly around Zoe like a savage swarm,

because I see, I know, that she will walk through them,
surrounded by a cloak of bright light,
so pure that she will not so much as notice them.

THEODORA: And will you leave this room, with me,
and leave Zoe alone with your deadly enemy?

TRAPEZOND: Princess: tell me, afterwards, how right I was to go.

ZOE: Don't go. I feel good, yes, but I'm afraid.
I hear a sound like the ringing of hundreds of faraway
   harps
and the wind burns me, it's too hot,
too heady—I feel like the clouds
that melt in a clear sky, at noon,
and I don't know what's happening to me.

THEODORA: [*To* Trapezond]
How powerfully you are loved. I can remember,
listening to her, my own dreams, as a girl.
Can you still doubt, can you possibly still doubt?
Then you're not worthy of her.

TRAPEZOND: I am worthy, and I shall go. Princess:
you're more sacred, to me, than the Holy Gifts.
Christ will smile a radiant smile
When you enter his white paradise.
[*Exeunt* Trapezond *and* Theodora. *Enter* Imru]

Scene v. Imru *and* Zoe

ZOE: Don't come near me, don't come near me.
Please: don't speak to me.
Your strange country, what is it to me—
or your fate, your sad fate.
I didn't tear down your father's house,
I only saw you in a dream.

IMRU: Princess!

ZOE: No, be still, be still, be still.
Your voice reminds me of something
I should have forgotten long ago.

IMRU: My father's house has been burned down,
         my people are hunted, we are few
         —and you, you, whose lips are sweeter than honey,
         you have chosen to stand with my enemies.
         I will leave.
                      [*Starts to leave, but then comes closer*]

ZOE: But you were going to ride away,
         you were going to ride after vengeance:
         they said you were.

IMRU: I will never see the desert, or the sea:
         the king of Trapezond is to be the general
         —is to be your husband—and I
         will be rewarded with chains, with a prison cell,
         for having seen you, once, for having
         Caught a single look from your eyes.

ZOE: Do you think I'm guilty?

IMRU: You are, yes! You're guilty of this terrible, this fierce
           love,
         you're guilty of your blinding beauty,
         and of your dazzling body—you're guilty, yes.

ZOE: Be still, oh, be still. I've been dreaming
         for too long, and dreaming uselessly, of words like
           these.
         Why have you come here to confuse me
         with your sadness, your beauty, your passion?

IMRU: What are all my oaths worth? What are the many roads
         that lead back to my own country?
         Only in you can I find
         the delights of heaven.

ZOE: Go away, go away. I don't love you,
         I will never love you.
         You frighten me, your words
         burn me, they make me feel no tenderness.

IMRU: [*Embracing her*]
         Is the female eagle tender to her mate
         when their marriage is performed, high under the
           shelter
         of a cloud? No:

passion will tear through the agonizing mist
across your eyes—like lightning.

ZOE: I'm to be married: you know that.
I don't belong to myself, I belong to him.
Think, oh, think: I'm the emperor's daughter,
the only heir to the mighty throne of Byzantium—
but you're not listening.
And as soon as I say these things
I forget them—
oh, why have the walls moved so far away,
why is the sky here, burning with light,
with hot bright light?
I'm a tiny cloud, you're the free wind,
playing with me as you please.
Look: an angel is bending down, he's watching,
my guardian angel, my friend when I played children's
    games.
Angel—why is he so sad?—angel, dear angel,
I'm only a tiny cloud, I feel so weightless, so light, so
    sweet.
                [Imru *carries her off*]

ACT IV

Scene i. Imru *and the* Eunuch

EUNUCH: Well, how did you sleep, in your new
quarters? Strange,
I'm sure, to wake
without your Arab woman beside you,
in a bed that had no scent of camel sweat
and no hyena howling outside the window.

IMRU: I spent the whole night in strange and wonderful
    visions,
my soul on an executioner's rack.
An eagle circled high in a sky I did not know,
screaming like the clanging of swords.
And then, through the crashing of steel, I would hear,
tearing through, a piercing cry, inconsolable—
and there was a strange lightning . . .

and a piercing cry . . . and my heart leaped like a ball.
Shame was there, dark and as inevitable as death,
more oppressive even than death.
Shame skulked along dark alleys,
following the footsteps of the woman I loved.
—And I woke up. The morning was too bright,
the air was heavy with roses.
But this terrible, beautiful dream did not come to me
for no reason—I know that.

EUNUCH: Of course not. The empress has ordered
freedom for you,
but only until noon. And then you'll be chained,
and there'll be no roses and no sun either.
The imperial command must be obeyed.

IMRU: Oh chance, as all-powerful as Nature herself,
flying here and there as you please,
I fall at your feet, now,
not for myself,
not for my people,
but only for her who, like a lightning flash,
lit this agonizing passion inside me—
only for her, O gay dancer, O chance,
only for her show your divine power.

EUNUCH: How amusing, these prayers of yours. I love
such interwound, subtle syllogisms—I really do.
That's the common game, in Egypt:
the Greeks there, and the Phoenicians, and the Arabs
        too,
take logical figures
and geometrical juxtapositions
and spin out faiths no one has ever heard of,
and which live, like moths,
for a single day—but which are charming, fascinating.
Have you been there, by some chance?

IMRU: I've lived in Alexandria.
Fifteen years ago.

EUNUCH: Exactly when Theodora was there.

IMRU: Which Theodora?

EUNUCH:	Don't tell me you're ignorant Of our empress' name!
IMRU:	Theodora? With hair black as pitch, with light feet whiter than cedar nuts fresh from their shell, with a hot mouth? Ha, ha—I'm saved, I'm saved!
EUNUCH:	No, you couldn't have met her, she lived in the desert, learning repentance and prayer from an old hermit— and you, you were surely swilling in the palaces of rich merchants and army officers, going to the games, hunting animals, attending pagan schools. However, it will be midday shortly, and time for us to go off— and the empress will be here, this is her usual time.
IMRU:	She's exactly who I need to see. [Imru *leaps on the* Eunuch, *forces him down, ties his clothes over his head, then straightens and waits*]

Scene ii. Imru *and* Theodora

THEODORA:	[*As she enters*] You're still here?
IMRU:	I'm here, Empress, to thank you, and also to arrange the details of my marriage to Princess Zoe.
THEODORA:	Ah, poor man, you've gone mad.
IMRU:	[*Continuing*] And to arrange, also, that I, not the king of Trapezond, will be the general for the Arabian expedition.
THEODORA:	Why aren't you lying in chains? Where's that lazy eunuch?

IMRU: [*Pointing*]
                 Here. He's right here, where I tied him up
                 and left him. He was boring me, bothering me.

THEODORA: How dare you, you beggar without a name,
                 to do violence to a man with a noble post?
                 No: this is too much—out there: Guards! Guards!
                 Come here, at once!

IMRU: Tell me, Theodora:
                 does the birthmark under your left breast
                 still look like a little mouse?
                 It used to.

THEODORA: What are you talking about?

IMRU: Do you see this scar?
                 Remember, one warm, moonlit night,
                 back in Alexandria, when you bit me
                 while you were dancing in front of us
                 and I threw you my purse—
                 with diamonds in it, do you remember? Diamonds,
                     not just gold.

THEODORA: You? Are you that Imru? What black magic!
                 What are you doing here?—do you realize,
                 Imru,
                 that you were the only one I loved?

IMRU: Not really, no! There were a lot of your lovers
                 in Alexandria.

THEODORA: There was no pleasure in it, before I met you.
                 I gave myself innocently, like a child—
                 the memory tortures me!
                 Do you still love me?

IMRU: No.

THEODORA: I see. An unripe little bitch
                 with big eyes and a sad mouth
                 means more to you—she'll die, I'll kill her!

IMRU: Empress: it's sad, having to live in chains.

THEODORA: In chains?

IMRU: In chains, yes. If the emperor learns what I know,
                 do you think he'll forgive you?

THEODORA: And you're quite determined to betray a woman
with whom you once knew delight?

IMRU: My fate is forever linked with Zoe's,
I have to save her.

THEODORA: And what do you want me to do?

IMRU: To accept the situation: that's all.
Sometimes, after a thief has knocked a traveller off a
bridge, down into a river, he jumps in and
pulls him out, suddenly realizing that
his victim was an old friend.

THEODORA: You'll have your vengeance, but I won't have mine.

IMRU: I was lucky. I deserved it.

THEODORA: That's how it goes, isn't it?
Well, my heart has started up again—
beating without hatred, without love, just
following the tambourine
and the swift-flying feet
and the arms, thrown high like flower stems.
I didn't dance badly, did I?

IMRU: Good luck, Theodora. You heard what I said,
I'm going—but remember:
treachery doesn't work, not with me.
                    [*Pointing to the* Eunuch]
Should I slit his throat?
He's heard what we said.

THEODORA: It's not worth it.
He'll hold his tongue: he knows so many secrets
already that they don't interest him.
But take him away, quickly:
the emperor is coming.
                    [Imru *carries the* Eunuch *off*]

Scene iii. Theodora *and* Justinian

JUSTINIAN: [*Entering*]
Who was that, with you just now?

THEODORA: The Arab.

JUSTINIAN:	But—what was he doing?
THEODORA:	Talking to me.
JUSTINIAN:	Has he been freed? How?
THEODORA:	At my order, confirmed by this ring.
JUSTINIAN:	[*Pulling the ring away*] Give it back, give it back to me.
THEODORA:	Take it. But I did the right thing: he would have been dangerous, here in Byzantium, even in prison.
JUSTINIAN:	Dangerous? To whom?
THEODORA:	To me, only to me!
JUSTINIAN:	What are you saying? What? Has he tried to kill you?
THEODORA:	Can't you see how my face is burning, don't you see how hard it is to talk of this—with you? I'm so ashamed! You're only jealous of sins I never committed: the real danger escapes your notice.
JUSTINIAN:	Do you love him? Did you give yourself to him?
THEODORA:	Ah no: had I given myself to him where would I have found the strength to confess?
JUSTINIAN:	Then what's wrong?
THEODORA:	I'm thirty years old, my Emperor, and at that age women experience temptations they've never known in all their lives. If you send him to prison, here, my mind will always turn to prison thoughts, every rustle, every sound will seem to me like the chains ringing on his lovely bronze legs. If you kill him, ah, the pain will be worse. Once dead, he'll begin to appear to me, at night, to caress me—and his agonizing kisses

will reek of decay.
Oh my husband, I've loved you
like glorious pearls, like the star of the East,
like the fragrant rose—and you
want to betray me, to hand me
over to a cunning serpent.

JUSTINIAN: I believe you. I always believe you
when you accuse yourself . . .

THEODORA: My Emperor:
there is a way to protect me
from these tortures, this fantastic, this unheard-of
    disgrace.
Let him be the general, let him command
the Arabian expedition.
Once I know that he is happy,
that he will never return to Byzantium,
my passion will fade away like the shadow
of a cloud, melted by the sun.

JUSTINIAN: I've given that command
to the king of Trapezond. It's easier
to take food from a hungry lion
than war from a soldier like him.

THEODORA: It will not be so difficult: Zoe
can manage him.

JUSTINIAN: Why Zoe? Has that Arab
bewitched her, as he has you?

THEODORA: I'm thirty, Emperor, and she is thirteen.
Consider what you're saying.

JUSTINIAN: Forgive me.
How happy I am to hear you
telling the truth, to hear you
defending Zoe to me.
So be it, then!

THEODORA: Oh, glorious, wonderful Emperor!
You have saved me, and I love you.
        [*Exeunt. Enter* Trapezond *and* Zoe]

Scene iv. Trapezond *and* Zoe

TRAPEZOND: How happy I am, Zoe! You and I
are closer, dearer to one another. But
still, there is something we need to talk about:
that Arab. Was he frightened?
Did he bow down before you?

ZOE: Yes.

TRAPEZOND: And what did you say to him?

ZOE: I said nothing.

TRAPEZOND: And him?

ZOE: He said nothing.
Only,
the stars sang so clearly in the drowsy sky,
and a wingèd angel bent over me
and wept.
—Listen:
I slept with the Arab.

TRAPEZOND: You can't—you don't know what you're saying.

ZOE: I've never pretended
that I loved you: why does this hurt me so?
And you'll forgive me, won't you?

TRAPEZOND: Princess: don't test my love.
I can't stand a test like this.

ZOE: Don't torture me, don't make me repeat
that terrible confession.

TRAPEZOND: How? How could this happen?

ZOE: I love him.

TRAPEZOND: A stranger, a beggar,
with a guttural voice, with morbid eyes,
with the character of a brave hyena,
without a shadow of a human soul?

ZOE: How dare you say such things!
He's as tender as the hot wind from the south,
his words ring in my heart like a lute,

	and only he understands my heart.
	And the kingdom he lost
	was so splendid that nowhere in Byzantium
	can we equal it—
	nowhere in Byzantium! And
	certainly not in your miserable Trapezond.
TRAPEZOND:	Forgive me! Even I, a soldier,
	forgot for a moment that the only right is victory.
ZOE:	You've hurt me, hurt me deeply, but
	I forgive you, because now you
	will help me. Why do you need another war?
	You have more than enough glory.
	Let him to whom that vengeance is dearest
	lead the army, let him be the general,
	let him take back his house, and his father's throne,
	so that I may become his wife.
TRAPEZOND:	And you ask me for that?
ZOE:	Has all your love for me
	vanished?
TRAPEZOND:	I remember an old proverb—
	I don't know where I heard it.
	It says that a woman is not simply human
	but half a gentle angel
	and half a ferocious demon, mysteriously joined
	together.
	And with the man she loves she is all angel,
	and with the man she doesn't love she is all demon.
ZOE:	You're reproaching me—again.
	And you haven't answered.
TRAPEZOND:	Answered what?
ZOE:	Will you let him be the general?
TRAPEZOND:	Are you still asking such things of me?
	My good sword is wide, and it gleams bright,
	but if I stare at it my sword will turn dull, now,
	and even that powerful horse I used to ride
	couldn't hold me, now, support this monstrous pain—
	Stop! Anyone who wants to can be the general.

ZOE: Oh, how your pain hurts me! I feel
                 that somehow I have been guilty!
                 I'll give you everything, everything: leave me only
                 my happiness and my love.

TRAPEZOND: Zoe: I need nothing else.

ACT V

Scene i. Imru *and* Zoe

IMRU: Princess: how fine! An order just came,
                 sealed with the emperor's own seal.
                 I'm to have fifteen thousand soldiers: archers,
                 cavalry, foot soldiers, and armed barbarians,
                 all ready, ready right now.
                 And I will lead them, I will lead them,
                 Princess.

ZOE: A little while ago you called me Zoe.

IMRU: Yes.
                 Forgive me, Princess: I was at the gates,
                 I saw a horse as big as a wild elephant,
                 as red as fire: that's
                 my horse. I went up to him and
                 he looked at me, sideways, vicious, oh how vicious!
                 I'll be riding on him, at the head
                 of an army like no one has ever seen, in all Arabia.

ZOE: You'll build your city again, won't you,
                 and in your palace fountains will flow all day and all
                     night
                 and roses as big as a child's head
                 will grow in front of the fountains,
                 won't they? And in the evening, in a palm grove,
                 we'll walk hand in hand, won't we, and birds,
                 oh such birds will sing, magic birds
                 as blue as moons, and my heart
                 will be afraid, as it was when you carried me,
                 but my guardian angel won't be sad anymore,
                 will he?

IMRU: Of course, of course! But first I'll pull down
          the Benu-Assad hornet's nest.
          I know where they ring their tents:
          I'll send the cavalry along the meadows, and
          the foot soldiers will take the left, just past the creek.
          When the Benu-Assad come down the ravine
          the archers up on the cliffs will pour down arrows
          like hail with feathers,
          and then my armed barbarians will finish them off,
          their eyes as cold as their country,
          their arms stronger than blacksmiths' hammers.

ZOE: And then you'll come back for me?

IMRU: Yes.
          Oh how happy I am! While I rode across the desert,
          coming here, the lovely wind from the south burned
             my face,
          waves arched up in the middle of the Bosphorus—
          maybe the same waves that beat up against
          the rocks of Africa, while lions, drunk
          with killing all night, stared down at their reflections.
          But you're sad. Are you sad?

ZOE: You're going,
          and it hurts me.

IMRU: I will come to you in your dreams, bloody
          —but it will be my enemies' blood, not mine.
          With a sharp, wry smile I'll show you
          the chopped-off heads of sheiks I hate,
          I'll hold them up by the hair,
          and then you'll realize that it was good
          that you pressed yourself against me, yesterday.

ZOE: But perhaps you could take me with you?
          Perhaps you could stay just a little longer?
          I have enemies.

IMRU: Don't let them frighten you!
          And who are they? The king of Trapezond is a soldier:
          he wouldn't hurt a woman.
          Justinian? He's your father. The eunuch?
          A fat old man who likes to make speeches.
          Ah yes: the empress Theodora.

Don't let her frighten you, not now:
I pulled some of that viper's teeth.
Let me tell you how to handle her—
[*He glances out the window*] What's that?
The soldiers are marching—there's the first column
boarding the first ship,
and I'm not there. Farewell, Princess:
it's time.

ZOE: One more second.

IMRU: There are the foot soldiers.
You can't see their faces, in the sunlight,
their armor glitters so bright.
I'm going.

ZOE: One kiss, just one kiss.

IMRU: There are my barbarians!
             [Imru *leaves*. Theodora *enters and stands
             watching, unnoticed by* Zoe]

Scene ii. Zoe *and* Theodora

ZOE: He's gone . . . like a dream, just before dawn,
he's gone . . . and he didn't kiss me.
He has bright roads in front of him,
and deserts, and oases, and oceans,
and war . . . but if he . . . no, no, I know
that's impossible . . . he'll come back, nothing
will hurt him, and he'll take me away
to white fountains and sacred roses.
             [*She looks out the window*]
There are soldiers going by, down there. He knows
which ones are archers, and foot soldiers, but I don't,
they all have such weathered faces,
and they walk so heavily, as if they'd just walked here
from France, without stopping,
and were planning to walk to India.
They're not talking, children run after them,
and those women in torn dresses
are snatching at their hands, and kissing them.
As I . . . as I wanted to kiss him.

They frighten me, those soldiers: they have bear skins
and tiger skins hanging from their shoulders,
their arms look like they're just part of their swords,
they just keep on and on, and they never lower their
    eyes,
they look straight ahead, they're not afraid, they
    believe,
like people who have nothing to be ashamed of
no treachery, no betrayals, no dishonesty at all.
Soldiers: keep your sacred courage, keep it,
watch over him, your general,
my belovèd.

THEODORA: Zoe!
Console yourself, my daughter. Your husband
is here, and today is your wedding.

ZOE: He stayed?

THEODORA: The Arab was the general.

ZOE: Then he's gone?

THEODORA: Zoe, Zoe!
The king of Trapezond is at the altar, waiting for you,
and you—may I say it—you are here, longing for the
    Arab.

ZOE: Imru al-Kais, ibn Hujir, will be my husband.
I want no other husband.
I will accept no other husband.

THEODORA: I'll say nothing against Imru—
Though he says things against me.—Doesn't he?
You're silent . . . I guess that means he did, he
talked to you about me, didn't he?
Well: the king was chosen for you by your father,
and you know your father,
he won't like having promised for nothing—
or having poisoned the tunic for nothing.

ZOE: Poisoned the tunic? What tunic? I don't understand.

THEODORA: The king of Trapezond's tunic,
his wedding present from the emperor.

ZOE: But why?

THEODORA: Because Trapezond is a coastal city
              and a very rich city,
              and you will be the queen of Trapezond.

ZOE: For me? To kill him,
              when I've hurt him so much,
              when I'd give my life to wipe out
              my guilt? . . . Oh how horrible!

THEODORA: About that, Zoe, you'll need to talk to your father.
              [*Enter* Justinian]

Scene iii. Zoe, Theodora, *and* Justinian

JUSTINIAN: It pleases me to see you two together. Peace
              in the emperor's own family is the sacred model
              of peace in the state.

THEODORA: Well, if that's how it is, then the people
              have risen in rebellion, and they're running across
              the city, howling, and the buildings
              are burning, the palaces are crumbling,
              and robbers and wolves are prowling under the walls,
              hunting happily.
              The princess refuses to do as you say.

ZOE: Father, is the marriage tunic really
              poisoned? Can it be?

JUSTINIAN: It is.

ZOE: But why?

JUSTINIAN: Why is there lightning in the sky,
              burning farmers' huts and their fields,
              why are there storms and burning desert winds,
              why are there poisonous flowers?
              My child, the laws of the state,
              the laws of human destiny
              here on this earth, where the Lord leads us
              along inscrutable pathways,
              are all the same, for creatures,
              for grass, for a grain of sand.

ZOE: I don't want him to die!

JUSTINIAN:	I'd thought you didn't love him, Zoe.
ZOE:	I don't want to marry him, but if he dies I'll die too!
JUSTINIAN:	Zoe: do you see? Your plans, your desires, are just as incomprehensible to me as mine to you—and therefore the Lord created blue-eyed obedience and calm faith, so people can live in harmony where there is no harmony—
ZOE:	Father, you're wise, you're learned, you're the emperor, the Lord's anointed: for you the paths of good and evil, of happiness and suffering, are woven together, and they lead you to the glory you'll receive in heaven. But I'm a girl, a young girl, and that's all I am! Let me be good, let me be happy!
JUSTINIAN:	My child: even for your happiness —and I swore to your dead mother, now a saint in heaven, that I would protect you —I cannot simply abandon my plans. But I'll change them. Only a vicious bull, finding an irresistible obstacle in front of him, cripples himself by battling with it. A wise man simply goes around and finds what he has wanted. The king of Trapezond will live, and you will not be his wife. Let a husband you want with your heart come to you. *[Enter the* Eunuch]

Scene iv. Zoe, Theodora, Justinian, *and the* Eunuch

EUNUCH:	O Born-to-the-Royal-Purple! Oh horrible, horrible, horrible! Better that I should kill myself than come to you bearing such news and cloud the princess Zoe's clear young eyes!
THEODORA:	Collect yourself! Grief is improper in an audience with your ruler.

JUSTINIAN: The sovereign ruler of this world is also a man,
and he does not stop the sorrowful from their tears.
Tell me: what happened?

EUNUCH: He was coming out of this hall, at midday
—the king of Trapezond—and
I met him,
and even though I hadn't yet eaten a thing
he took me by the hand and led me
around and around the cathedral of Saint Sophia.
He didn't speak—except once
he asked me if, as the Scythian tradition requires,
there was a man buried
under the foundations of the temple,
so the walls would stand stable
and the columns stand uncracked.
I crossed myself and told him
that this was a superstition unworthy
of both the emperor and of Byzantium.
He smiled a crooked smile, in the corners of his mouth,
and again he was silent.
O Born-to-the-Royal-Purple, you know the temple!
We climbed along narrow, shaky ladders, and across
footways that were only boards laid end to end,
up among monstrous scaffolding that seemed like the
    ribs
of Leviathan or Behemoth,
up to where the architect plans
to put an earthenware cupola.
He stood there, at that terrible height,
his face to the south and gilded by the sun—
he seemed like a spirit—and he began to talk.
I held onto the railing, and I listened.
He said—he said
that this city, and its buildings, and its palaces, and
its roadways were,
like all the words and desires and meditations
that rule over man,
the dead's legacy to the living.
He said that there were two worlds, two unequal
    worlds.

One of them, huge, very huge, held geniuses and
    heroes,
who fill the entire universe with glory.
And in the little world, he said, in the little one
are all the rest of us, pitiful descendants
of geniuses and heroes, slaves
of necessity and of fate.
And then he said—he said that death was not terrible,
that Herakles had died, and Julius Caesar had died,
and Mary had died, and Christ had died—
and suddenly, as he said Christ's name,
he stepped forward over the edge of the wall, where
    the air
hung bright with the midday sun . . .
I felt that he was standing high over an abyss,
that he had overcome all earthly weight,
and my head whirled, terribly, and I closed my eyes
for a second, for half a second,
and when I opened them again
—Oh Lord, Lord!—there was no one there.
How I got down those planked footways I don't know.
But down on the other side of the wall I heard
a crowd, excited, standing around a pile of meat and
    bones
that had no human shape.
Our stonemasons are hard people: they like
animal fights best of anything in the world,
and they fight among themselves, and they're often
    drunk,
but their weathered faces trembled
and there were tears in those black eyes
when I told them—and I was weeping too—
when I cried out that this, in front of them,
this was the king of Trapezond.
They loved him, he was gay
and he was brave, and he was handsome.
And I loved him for his lofty spirit
and because he could endure any pain.
And then—do I dare to say this?—oh then I heard
some of them muttering curses

and looking at the imperial palace.
They suspect secret things everywhere.

JUSTINIAN: This must be investigated at once:
everyone responsible is to be arrested!
Oh, I grieve for the king. And now Persia
will want Trapezond, I know it will.

ZOE: He lived for me, and he died. And I,
I, am his only murderer.

JUSTINIAN: My child: grief for your husband
has unhinged your mind.

ZOE: I'm a murderer! Didn't I see him
trembling, as I spoke,
like a miserable traveller, staggering
as robbers leap on him with drawn daggers?
Didn't I understand
that truth is an abomination, a loathsome abomination,
if there is no mercy mixed into it?
Oh how will I justify myself before God?
How will I explain this to Imru?

THEODORA: It was you who said it! Remember, remember
that I did not betray you!

JUSTINIAN: Betray what? What has Imru al-Kais got to do with
this?

ZOE: Father: father: no one but you
can understand me, console me, and forgive me.
Father: I wanted the Arab, not the king,
and I gave myself to him.
But how can I be the queen of Arabia,
how can I be happy among fountains and
palms, held in belovèd arms,
when I am stained with innocent blood?

JUSTINIAN: You,
heir to the throne of Byzantium,
you gave yourself to a wandering Arab?
Oh, the disgrace, the disgrace on my head—
and the misery for you, who have done this!
Call back the soldiers. At once.
The Arab is to be ripped apart on the rack. At once!

EUNUCH:	O Born-to-the-Royal-Purple, it's too late! The last ship has already sailed, I saw it leave.
JUSTINIAN:	Send a reliable messenger, order the Arab to return. At once.
EUNUCH:	At once, by my own hand.
THEODORA:	He won't come.
JUSTINIAN:	No? Then—then send him the wedding tunic as a sign of my imperial grace and good will to him. The tunic will be no better than the rack.
ZOE:	Father: what are you going to do with me, and with the man who is dearer to me, now, than life itself?
JUSTINIAN:	I will answer you. This is the last time I will ever speak to you. Repentance alone will never wash the disgrace from noble Roman blood. You will take the nun's habit, you will stay in your room, alone, until you die. And he will wear the wedding tunic, he will lift a cup and toast your beauty, but the cup will fall from his hands, and foam, not wine, will moisten his lips, he'll cry out, "What? What?" And then he'll answer himself with animal howling, over and over and over, and a dry fire will burn him to ashes, will break his bones, one by one, and tear his veins apart, and in the last second, as he dies, as he dies, he'll put a horrible curse on your name! [*To the* Eunuch] Come. [*To* Theodora] Stay with her, who was my daughter, once. Prepare her soul to be a nun! [*Exeunt* Justinian *and the* Eunuch]

Scene v. Theodora *and* Zoe

THEODORA: Neither of you can hurt me, now:
nuns don't talk,
and neither do corpses.
It's time for me to tell the truth, too,
the whole truth.
I've always hated you,
for your delicate hands, for your sad eyes,
for the calm languor
with which you moved and talked.
You've lived here like some exotic bird
extinct for centuries; even the palace slaves
talked about you and were uncomfortable.
Your blood is ancient Roman,
but mine is low, God only knows just who my
    grandfathers were.
And yesterday you were still a virgin,
and only angels bent over you,
and I know all the whorehouses, all the taverns, all the
    thieves' dens
in Constantinople, where knives are drawn over
    women,
where drunken sailors made love to me.
But I'm cleaner than you!
I stand and look at you,
and I feel horrified, I feel disgusted.
All the palace filth, all your ancestors' sins,
all the treachery of Byzantium, all its rottenness
is alive, now, in your unknowing, childish body—
as death lives, sometimes,
in a flower, as it grows out of a plague cemetery.
You think you're a woman—but you're
a poisoned wedding tunic,
every step you take is death, everywhere you look
you bring death!
The touch of your hand is death!
The king of Trapezond is dead,
Imru will soon be dead,

but you're still alive, fragrant with darkness.
Pray!
But your prayers frighten me,
they'd seem like blasphemy.

> [*Exit* Theodora. Zoe *stands, a few moments,
> then falls on her knees, her face on the
> ground. Curtain.*]

Literary Criticism

The Anatomy of a Poem

There are many definitions of the essence of poetry, but two—proposed by poets themselves, poets who had begun to think about the mysteries of their craft—stand out. Coleridge's formula runs, "Poetry is the best words in the best order." And Théodore de Banville's formula: "Poetry is that which has been created, and therefore does not need to be changed." Both these formulas are founded in a singularly clear awareness of the laws by which words influence our consciousness. A poet is a poet because he takes into consideration *all* the laws which govern the complex of words he has taken. To take into consideration only *part* of these laws is to be a writer of prose, an artist in prose; to take into consideration nothing but the ideological content of words and their combinations is to be a man of letters, a creator of business prose.

Enumerating and classifying these laws is the work of poetic theory. This theory must be deductive, and not based simply on the study of actual poetry—just as the art of mechanics *explains* various constructions, rather than only describing them. The theory of prose (if there can be any such thing), on the other hand, has no choice but to be inductive, describing how one or another prose writer in fact works. It would otherwise merge into and become poetic theory.

Further: as Potebnia has shown, poetry is a linguistic phenomenon, or, viewed slightly differently, a special form of speech. Now, all speech is addressed *to* someone, and it contains something which concerns both speaker and listener—the speaker thus attributing to the listener one or more characteristics which he knows he himself possesses. The human personality is capable of infinite subdivisions. Our words express only a part of us, one of our many faces. We can talk about our love, for example, to a woman we love, or to a friend, or we can talk about it in court, or in drunken company, or to flowers, or to God. Each time, clearly, the story will be different, since *we* are different, depending on the situation. And the listener, very similarly, has the same kind of multiformity—since what we speak to is only a single part of *him*. So, if we speak to the sea, we can be aware of how like ourselves it is or, inversely, how unlike. We can credit it with concern for us, or with indifference, or with hostility. (However, description of the sea from folkloristic, pictorial, or geological points of view, though this is often linked to manner of address, is in fact not relevant here, since, plainly, *that* form of address is no more than a device, the real person to whom we speak being—someone quite different.)

Every time we speak there is a volitional starting point; and the poet, to make his words work, must see very clearly what relation exists between speaker and person spoken to, and he must feel the conditions under which a connection between the two is really possible. This needs to be discussed as part of the broader subject of poetic psychology.

Both poetic psychology and poetic theory are in operation in all poetry. Poetic theory might be likened to anatomy, and poetic psychology to physiology. And the living poem is thus open to examination like any other viable organism, examination both anatomical and physiological.

Poetic theory can be divided into four main parts: phonetics, stylistics, composition, and imagery.

Phonetics looks into the acoustical side of verse, that is, the rhythm (the alternations in pitch and volume), the instrumentation (the quality of and the connections between various sounds), the nature of endings and the nature of rhyme—that is, the acoustical aspects of rhyme.

Stylistics considers the effects of words, depending on their origin, their age, their classification in one or another grammatical category, their functional role in a particular phrase, and also the effect of a group of words which are virtually a single word, for example, as metaphor, simile, etc.

Composition has to do with units of ideological ordering. It studies the intensity, and the shifting of thoughts, feelings, and images which have been put into a poem. Questions of form enter here, because a poet's choice of, say, one stanzaic form rather than another will vastly influence the poetic movement of his mind.

Imagery is a summation of poetry's themes and of the poet's possible relationships to those themes.

Each of these classifications passes unnoticed into the next—and imagery is very close indeed to poetic psychology. Sharp and clear lines cannot be drawn, and should not be drawn. In truly great poetry all four main classifications receive equal attention, and are thus mutually complementary. The poetry of Homer, for example, or *The Divine Comedy*. A large shift in poetic direction usually pays particular attention to some two of the chief classifications, blending them into one another and tending to ignore the other two. Minor shifts focus on only one of the major classifications, sometimes even just one device through which it operates. I should point out, incidentally, just in passing, that Acmeism, a movement born only in the last few years, makes as one of its principal demands the requirement that uniform attention be given to all four major classifications. (The French poets who belonged to the now-disintegrated group, L'Abbaye, made this same demand.) . . .

[A brief discussion of Russian religious verse, intended as an exemplar of Gumilev's method, is omitted here. It is too closely tied to Russian metrics and to the Russian language to make much sense to English-speaking readers. Gumilev then concludes:]

We trust that the time will come when poets will begin to weigh their every word with the same care employed by the creators of religious cult-songs!

On the Translation of Poetry

1

There are three ways to translate a poem.

First, the translator uses whatever meter, whatever rhyme scheme happens to come into his head; uses his own personal vocabulary (often alien to that used by the author); and, as he pleases, either lengthens or shortens the original. This is clearly amateurish translation, and only that.

Second, the translator *acts,* for the most part, in exactly the same way —but he produces some theoretical justification for what he has been up to, he assures us that if the poet being translated had written, instead, in Russian, he would have written just as the translator presents him. This was a very widespread method in the eighteenth century. Pope, in England, and Kostrov, here in Russia, translated Homer this way, and both enjoyed extraordinary success. The nineteenth century basically rejected this method, but we still see surviving traces of it. And there are still those who believe it perfectly proper to substitute one meter for another (for instance, a five-footed metric for a six-footed one), to forego rhyming, to introduce new images, and so on. The idea is that the spirit is preserved, and that this justifies everything.

However—and this is the third approach to translating a poem—any poet worthy of the name uses exactly this discarded form as his sole method of expressing his spirit. And I will now attempt to outline how this is accomplished.

2

The first thing a reader notices, and what very probably seems to him the most important (though often an unconscious) basis for a poem, is its idea—or, more exactly, its image, since a poet thinks in images. The total number of images is limited, since they are drawn from actual life and the poet is rarely their creator. But only in his relationship to images does his personality come clear. For example, the Persian poets thought of the rose as a living being; medieval poets thought it the symbol of love and beauty; for Pushkin, a rose is a beautiful flower on its stem; for Maikov a rose is always a decoration, an accessory; for Vyacheslav Ivanov the rose becomes a thing of mystic value; and so on. Of course, in all these cases both the choice of individual words and the combinations of words are essentially different. And within the boundaries of the same relationship there is room for thousands of nuances: so Byron's Corsair's remarks, speaking about the background of his author's psychologically flowery description of him, stand out in sharp contrast with their laconic tone and their technical expressions. In his gloss to "The Raven," Edgar Poe talks about an undercurrent theme—that is, a theme barely marked out, and for that very reason creating a powerful effect. Suppose someone, translating that same "Raven," were to transmit with infinite care the external plot, the movements of the bird, and devote much less care to the poet's anguish over his dead beloved, the translation would transgress against the author's conception, and would not in fact be a translation.

3

Immediately after the choice of image, the poet needs to consider its development, its proportions. These determine the poem's length, and also the form, the stanza, in which it will be written. Here, the translator has no choice but to follow the author—blindly. It is not possible to shorten or to lengthen a poem without simultaneously changing its tone, even if one manages to retain the same number of images. Both the pithiness and the amorphousness of the image are part of the poet's intention, of his conception of the poem, and each line added or subtracted changes the degree of tension accorded that intention.

As far as stanza form is concerned: each one creates a particular train of thought, unlike other trains of thought. The sonnet, for example, stating a position in the first quatrain, moves to its antithesis in the second quatrain, then outlines the interaction of these two positions in the first tercet, and finally, in the second tercet, comes to some unexpected solution, condensed into the very last line, often even into the very last word—which is for that precise reason known as the key to the sonnet form. The Shakespearian sonnet, in which the rhyme does not run from one quatrain to the next, is supple, flexible, but insufficiently strong; the Italian sonnet, using only feminine end rhymes, is powerfully lyrical and very stately, but not well suited for telling a story or presenting a description—the usual form does better, in these cases. In the oriental *ghazal* form, the same word, and sometimes the same phrase, is repeated at the end of every line (incorrectly broken into two lines by Europeans), thus giving an impression like a gaily colored ornament, or an incantation. The octave form, extensive and spacious like no other form, is admirable for calm and unhurried narration. Even such ordinary forms as the quatrain and the couplet each have their own individual traits, which the poet takes into account, even if only unconsciously. And in any case, to really know a poet we must know what forms he preferred and how he used them. And therefore the translator is obliged to preserve his poet's forms exactly as they appear in the original.

4

As to style, the translator needs to master his author's poetics: each poet has his personal vocabulary, and often has theoretical reasons for his choice. Wordsworth, for example, insists on the necessity for colloquial language. Victor Hugo insists on using words in their direct senses. José-Maria de Heredia insists on precision. Verlaine, on the contrary, insists on the simplicity and casualness of language—and so on. It is particularly important that the translator understand the quality, the character of the original poet's comparisons. Thus, Byron is fond of comparing concrete images with abstract ones (remember the famous example in Lermontov, "the air is as fresh and pure as an infant's kiss"); Shakespeare prefers to compare the abstract with the concrete (as in Pushkin's famous "a beast with sharp claws, gnawing at the heart like conscience"); Heredia compares the concrete with the concrete ("like a flock of falcons flown down from their native cliffs . . . the warriors and captains said farewell to Palos"); Coleridge draws his comparisons from the number of images available to him, naturally and inevitably, because of the particular subject matter of a particular drama ("and each soul sang, like that arrow of mine"); in Edgar Poe the comparison turns into the development of the image; and so on. Poets use parallelisms, complete repetitions, inverted repetitions, shortened repetitions, exact indications of time or place, direct quotations woven into the text, and many other devices, each of which has a special hypnotic effect on the reader. I recommend that these be painstakingly preserved, sacrificing less important things if necessary. Further, many poets have paid great attention to the semantics of rhyme. Théodore de Banville, indeed, even argued that rhyme words are the most basic in a poem, are dominant, and are the first to arise in the poet's consciousness; they comprise, he asserted, the poem's skeleton—and for this reason it is desirable that at least one of the words in each rhymed pair be the same as one rhyme-word in the same pair in the original.

Most translators need to be warned about the use of such particles as *already, only, after all,* and so on. These all possess a mighty expressiveness, and usually double the verb's effective power. One can avoid them by choosing synonyms—there are a great many such possibilities in Russian. [Half a dozen examples, intelligible only in Russian, are omitted here.]

It is proper to use Slavisms, or archaisms, but only with great caution and when translating either the older poets, those who preceded Wordsworth and his Lake School, and the Romantics more generally, or else stylists like William Morris, in England, and Jean Moréas.

5

The acoustical side of poetry, finally, is the hardest of all for the translator to transmit. Russian syllabic verse is still too imperfectly worked out to use in the re-creation of French rhythms; English verse allows an arbitrary mixing of masculine and feminine rhymes, impermissible (or at least unnatural) in Russian. Relative transmission becomes necessary: turn syllabic verse into iambs, from time to time intermixing trochees; introduce regular alternation of rhymes into English poetry being translated, when possible using only masculine rhymes, more characteristic of the Russian language. But even this relative transmission must be strictly held to, because it was not created haphazardly and, for the most part, it really does give an adequate impression of the original.

Every meter has its own soul, its own peculiarities, its own purposes. The iamb—like going down a flight of stairs (the accented syllable being lower in pitch than the unaccented one)—is free, clear, firm, and beautifully transmits human speech, the tenseness of the human will. The trochee, a rising meter, is winged, always agitated, now emotional, now breaking into laughter. Its proper area is—song. The dactyl, supporting itself on the first, the accented, syllable, and rocking the two unaccented ones as a palm tree waves its high frond, is powerful, solemn, speaking of the elements and their peace, of gods and of heroes. Its opposite, the anapest, is impetuous, gusty; it is the elements in motion, the tension of inhuman passion. And the amphibrach [a trisyllabic foot: unstressed, stressed, and unstressed syllables, in that order], which is their synthesis, is lulling, transparent; it speaks of the peace of an existence divinely light and wise. And the properties of these metrics require that they be used differently, when they are used in different lengths. Iambic *tetrameter,* for example, is most often used for lyric narration; iambic *pentameter* is most often used for epics, or for dramatic narration; iambic *hexameter* is used for discursive verse; and so on. Poets often quarrel with these inherent formal properties, demanding other possibilities of them, and sometimes in fact they prevail. But such a struggle never fails to leave its traces in the poem's image, and these traces must, therefore, be preserved in the translation, strictly following the meters and the measure.

Rhyme is a subject that has much concerned poets. Voltaire demanded acoustical rhyme; Théodore de Banville required visual rhyme; Byron cheerfully rhymed personal names and used compound rhymes; the Parnassian poets used *rimes riches*—and Verlaine did just the opposite, using suppressed rhyme; the Symbolist poets often use assonance. The translator needs to know just what his author was up to, and then needs to follow him exactly.

Also of great importance is enjambement, the run-over line. Classical poets like Corneille and Racine did not permit this; the Romantics brought it into general use; the modernists have taken it to extremes. In this, too, the translator should be careful of his author's particular approach.

Clearly, from all that has been said, the translator of poetry must himself be a poet—and also a careful investigator and an honest, sensitive critic, who can choose an author's basic characteristics and, when he needs to, can sacrifice to these characteristics others of lesser importance. And he must forget his own personality, must think only of the author's personality. Ideally, translations should be presented unsigned.

To improve the technique of verse translation, one can do still more: the rhymes of the original can be carefully preserved; syllabic verse can be rendered in Russian syllabics; characteristic speech can be transmitted—Kipling's military language, Laforgue's Parisian jargon, Mallarmé's syntax, and so on.

I am, of course, not now referring to the ordinary translator, who need not attempt such improvements. But, briefly, let me repeat what *is* obligatory.

1. The number of lines must be unchanged.
2. The meter and the measure must be unchanged.
3. Alternation of rhymes must be followed exactly.
4. Enjambement, if used, must be carefully observed.
5. The nature of the rhymes must be strictly followed.
6. The character of the vocabulary must be adhered to.

7. The type of comparisons must be carefully reproduced.
8. Other peculiar devices must be observed.
9. Transitions in tone must be followed.

These are the translator's nine commandments. Since there is one less than Moses required, I hope these can be better observed.

For an emphatically different approach to the problems of translation, see Raffel, *The Forked Tongue: A Study of the Translation Process* (The Hague: Mouton, 1971).

Review of Andrey Biely (*Urn,* Moscow, 1909)

Of the whole generation of older Symbolists, Andrey Biely is the least cultured. Not in the literary culture of scholars—something like a Siamese medal, valued only because it is hard to get and not many people have one. In that culture Biely is strong; he can write, if he pleases, about "the Marburg philosopher" or "the golden triangle of Khiram." No: least cultured in the real culture of mankind, which teaches respect and self-criticism; which enters into the flesh and the blood and puts its stamp on every idea one thinks, every movement one makes. It does not seem, somehow, that Biely has ever been in the Louvre, or that he has ever read Homer . . . And I am not forming this judgment on the basis of his poems, "Ashes," or "A Goblet of Snowstorms"—God is their judge—but on the basis of all his literary activities, which I have been following for a long time, and following with real interest. And just why I say "with interest" will be clear in a moment.

As a poet, Biely quickly mastered all the fine points of contemporary versification and technique—just as a barbarian quickly agrees that fish is not eaten with a knife, colored collars are not for winter use, sonnets are not written with nineteen lines (as, incidentally, one not-unknown poet did recently write a sonnet). Biely uses free verse, and alliteration, and internal rhyme. Ah, but write an ordinary, regular poem, with precise and meaningful images, and without all the racket of superfluous words—*that* he cannot do. He is the inferior, in this, even to long-buried, third-rate poets like Benediktov, Mey, or Karolina Pavlova. And one could argue, strongly, that he has in fact no real understanding of iambic tetrameter—the meter in which almost all of *Urn* is written. After Pushkin had developed the iamb, that great master tended more and more to use the fourth paeon [three unstressed syllables, followed by a stressed syllable] as a variant which added the greatest sonority to his poetry. It is inconceivable that Biely abstains from so vital a method for revivifying his frequently wooden verse.

But what is Biely's charm—why are we drawn to thinking and talking about him? Because his work has motifs, and these motifs are, in sober truth, deep and unusual. He has enemies—time and space. He has friends—eternity, the final goal. He makes these abstract concepts concrete, he opposes them to his own personal *I;* they are, for him, real beings in a real world. Blending the too-airy colors of our older poets with the oppressively heavy and harsh colors of our contemporary poets, he achieves astonishing effects—and proves that his dream world is truly a splendid one:

> Red satin roses,
> a sad crystal fountain . . .

My readers will not be happy with this review. They will want to know, surely, whether I am praising or abusing Andrey Biely. I won't answer that question, however. The hour for adding up totals hasn't yet come.

Review of Fyodor Sologub
(*Sobranie Sochinenii,* vols. 1 and 5)

Sologub has written a great deal, but perhaps even more has been written about him. It may well be superfluous, at this point, to write still more. But whenever I read critiques of Sologub's work I find myself asking strange questions, so simply formulated as to be quite out of place. I find myself saying, really? Gogol's successor? But he's created no real school. A refined stylist? But most of his poems are so alike that you can hardly tell one from the other. A mighty visionary? But all we can remember, from out of his visions, is the Nedotykomka [a haunting vision, in Sologub's novel, *The Little Demon*], the Dog, and the star Mair! I can't explain this, and I don't intend to try, but I do want to try to examine Sologub's poetry from the same kinds of perspectives, and with the same standards in mind, with which one looks in general at a poet's work.

Sologub's images—but what kind of images can there be, if the poet has decreed that there is only *I,* and that this is the sole reality, and that this *I* is what has created the world? Who could be surprised, then, that his world is nothing more than a desert, containing nothing worthy of love—because to love means to feel something higher and better than oneself in something or someone else, and for Sologub this is, by definition, impossible. The poet looks out at his world as if seeing it through glass blackened with smoke. It has no colors; the lines, too, are somehow suspiciously rubbed out. Dawn-light is cold and sad, in Sologub; life is pale, the day clear, the abyss mute. His vocabulary is noble —yes, but how inexpressive. Compare it with even the vocabulary of Bryusov, or Balmont—and I won't go so far as to mention Ivanov, or Annensky, where the adjectives have such depth and color that they overwhelm the nouns.

His reluctance to mold and shape is especially plain in Sologub's rhymes. Rhyme, after all, is to a poem as the angle is to plastic art. It's the transition from one line to another, and must therefore be outwardly unexpected, internally well grounded, free, delicate, and resilient. But Sologub rhymes identical forms of verbs and rhymes adjectives too; without intending to, he plucks the wings from off his verse.

Sologub's strength as a poet lies in this: he has been, and he has remained, the only absolutely consistent decadent in our literature. Everything that wounds a morbid consciousness is cut out of his poetry; his images are utterly transient, they disappear, evaporate, leaving behind a barely audible melody, perhaps just a faint fragrance. To accomplish this he does not draw things as he in fact sees them; his greatest love is for "that which never was nor will be on earth." His Muse is "the Angel of dreams never seen on roads never travelled," a Muse who holds in his hands, like a knight's shield painted with his coat of arms, "the unread book that holds a forbidden secret." But most of all, of course, he loves to talk about death, this great poet-mystifier who seems never to have died—though he likes to assert the contrary.

About Nekrasov

[In 1921—the year of Gumilev's death—Korney Chukovsky submitted a questionnaire to a number of prominent poets, asking about their attitude to Nekrasov and to his poetry.]

1. Do you like Nekrasov's poetry?
   Yes. Very much.
2. Which of his poems do you consider his best?
   The epic-monumental ones: "Vlas," "The Admiral Is a Widower," "General Fyodor Karlych von Stube," the description of Tarbagatai in "To Grandfather," "Princess Trubetskaia"—and others.
3. What do you think of his versification and technique?
   Remarkably deep breathed; he controls the image he chooses; remarkable phonetics—really, continuing Derzhavin, as it were, right over Pushkin's head.
4. Wasn't there a time when his poetry meant more to you than the poetry of Pushkin and Lermontov?
   My youth, age fourteen to age sixteen.
5. As a child, how did you feel about Nekrasov?
   I hardly knew his poetry, then, and what I did know I despised for its estheticism.
6. As a youth, how did you feel about Nekrasov?
   He awakened in me the notion that a person could be in active relation to society. He awakened in me an interest in revolution.
7. Was Nekrasov's influence important in your creative work?
   No, unfortunately.
8. How do you feel about Turgenev's well-known assertion that "poetry did not even spend a night" in Nekrasov's verse?
   A prose writer is no judge of a poet.

Acmeism and the Legacy of Symbolism

Attentive readers can now see that Symbolism has finished its arc of development and is falling. For one thing, works of the Symbolist school are few and far between these days—and those that do appear are extremely feeble, even from the Symbolist point of view. And for another thing, more and more voices can be heard, more and more frequently, suggesting that standards and reputations which were unquestionable, not so very long ago, must now be reconsidered. And then, too, we now see Futurists, Ego-Futurists, and all the other hyenas that always follow in a lion's tracks. (The reader must not feel that, with this phrase, I'm burying all the extreme trends in contemporary art. Indeed, in an issue of *Apollon,* very shortly, we will devote an article to their examination and evaluation.) Replacing Symbolism there is a new trend—and the name is not important. Call it Acmeism (from the Greek *akmê,* meaning "the highest degree of something," "a blossom," "a time of blossoming"), or call it Adamism (a manly, clear, firm view of life)—whatever it may be called, a new trend that demands more balance, more precise knowledge of the relationships between subject and object, than Symbolism ever possessed. And yet for this trend to become fully and firmly established, for it to be a worthy successor to what preceded it, it must accept the latter's legacy, it must answer all the questions its predecessor posed. There is a responsibility in taking on the glory of one's forefathers—and Symbolism was a worthy father.

French Symbolism, which was the ancestor of all Symbolism in all countries, pushed purely literary problems to the foreground: free verse; a more distinctive and unstable style; metaphor above all else; and its notorious "theory of correspondences." [See, in particular, Baudelaire's sonnet, "Correspondences."] This theory fairly proclaims its non-French nature, and thus the non-national, alluvial sort of soil from which it was nurtured. The French spirit is far too devoted to the element of *light*—which separates and divides objects, which draws lines clearly, precisely, and in full detail. But Symbolism, on the other hand, mixes together all images and all things, emphasizes their changeability— and so could only have been born in the misty darkness of the German forests. A mystic might well say that French Symbolism was a direct result of France's defeat by the Germans, at Sedan. But simultaneously it has also uncovered, in French literature, an aristocratic thirst for the rare and the difficult—and this has saved it from the threat of a vulgar naturalism.

We Russians must take French Symbolism into account, if only because the new trend I spoke of, above, gives a decided preference to the French as against the Germanic spirit. Just as the French sought a new, a freer verse, so the Acmeists want to break the chains of meter by skipping syllables and, more than ever before in Russian, by freely transposing stresses. There are already poems written according to a newly rethought syllabic system of versification. The giddiness of Symbolism's metaphors got us used to bold turns of thought; the instability of our vocabulary led us to seek new words, with a more stable content, and to seek such words in the living speech of ordinary people. And a bright irony, which could not help but appear from time to time in French writers—an irony which nevertheless did not undermine the roots of our faith—has now replaced that hopeless Germanic seriousness which our Symbolists so love. And finally, while we warmly appreciate the Symbolists for pointing out to us the true significance of the symbol, we are not willing to sacrifice other poetic methods to it; we seek the full harmonization of all methods. This is, indeed, our answer to the "beautiful difficulty" question, now being discussed by both trends: it is harder, much harder, to be an Acmeist than to be a Symbolist—just as it is harder to build a temple than a tower. And one of the principles of the new trend is, precisely, always to take the line of greatest resistance.

German Symbolism, in the persons of Nietzsche and Ibsen, its fathers, put forward the question of man's role in the universe—the role of the individual in society—and solved the riddle by discovering some sort of objective goal, a dogmatic religious precept, which man was supposedly meant to serve. This proved that, for German Symbolism, each individual phenomenon did not have intrinsic worth, a worth which needs no external justification. For us, however, the hierarchy of phenomena is, simply, each individual phenomenon's own specific weight. We hold, too, that the weight of the most insignificant phenomenon is still immeasurably greater than the absence of weight—i.e., non-existence—so that, in the face of non-existence, all phenomena are brothers.

We would not dare to force the atom to bow to God, if this were not natural to it. But being aware of ourselves as phenomena among phenomena, we begin to participate in the world's rhythm, we accept all the forces which act upon us and, in our own turn, we create forces ourselves. It is our duty, our freedom, our joy, and our tragedy to guess, hourly, what the next hour may be for us, for our affairs, for the whole world—and to hurry that next hour forward. And what appears to us the highest reward is our dream of the final hour of all—which never stops our attention for even an instant—and which is a dream that will never come to pass. But to rebel, in the name of other conditions of existence, here in this world where we have death, seems to us as strange as a prisoner breaking down a wall when, right in front of him, there is an open door. Ethics turns into esthetics, here, spreading and broadening. And the highest strain of individualism creates community, and God becomes the Living God, because man has suddenly felt himself worthy of such a God. Death is then the curtain which separates us, the actors, from our audience, and in the inspiration of performance we disdain that cowardly peeping into the future, that contemptible inquiry, "What will happen next?" As Adamists we are in part like forest animals—and in any case we have no intention of surrendering the animal part of ourselves in return for neurasthenia.

But it's time for Russian Symbolism to come to the fore, in this essay.

Russian Symbolism directed its main energies into the sphere of the unknown. It fraternized first with mysticism, then with theosophy, then with occultism; some of its questing search almost turned into myth-making. And this Russian Symbolism has the right to ask Acmeism, its successor, whether all *it* can boast of is its animalism, and what attitude this new trend has toward the unknowable. The first thing Acmeism can answer is this: the unknowable, by simple definition, cannot be known. And second, it can say that all attempts of that sort are unchaste. The whole beauty, the whole sacred meaning of the stars lies precisely in their being infinitely far from the earth; no advance in aviation will ever change that. Only a poor imagination sees the evolution of the human personality always and only set in time and in space. How can we remember previous existences (if that is not a patently literary procedure), those times when we were in the abyss with myriads of other possibilities for existence, possibilities about which we know nothing except, indeed, that they do exist? After all, each such existence is negated by our existence; in its turn, each such existence negates our existence. The sense of not knowing ourselves, a feeling of childlike wisdom which is sweet to the point of pain—this is what the supernatural gives us. François Villon, asking where the most beautiful women of antiquity are now, answers himself with this mournful exclamation, "Mais où sont les neiges d'antan!" ("But where are the snows of yester-year!") And we feel, in this, the sense of the unearthly, the mysterious, far more keenly than in whole volumes which discuss at great length which side of the moon houses the souls of the dead . . . The principle of Acmeism: remember the existence of the unknowable, always remember it—but do not insult your thinking about it with more or less likely guesses. We do not reject the opportunity, when we have it, to show the soul trembling as it approaches another—but then we show it shuddering, and no more than that. Knowledge of God, of course, the beautiful Lady Theology, remains on her throne; the Acmeists do not want to bring her down to literature's level, nor do they want to raise literature into her diamond-like cold. And angels, and demons, and elemental and other spirits are now simply part of the material with which the artist works; they no longer need to have specific gravity greater than the other images which he chooses.

Any literary trend will find itself passionately devoted to certain writers, to certain literary epochs. Affection for the dead ties people more closely together than does any other single thing. In circles close to Acmeism, the names most frequently heard are Shakespeare, Rabelais, Villon, and Théophile Gautier. This is not an arbitrary selection. Each of these men is a cornerstone for the edifice of Acmeism, a high tension of one or another of its elements. Shakespeare showed us man's inner world; Rabelais showed us the body and its joys, a wise physicality; Villon told us about a life which hasn't the slightest doubt about itself, even though it knows everything—God, sin, death, immortality; Théophile Gautier found worthy garments of irreproachable forms for this life, and found them in art. To unite in oneself these four moments—this is the dream which is now uniting the people who so boldly call themselves Acmeists.